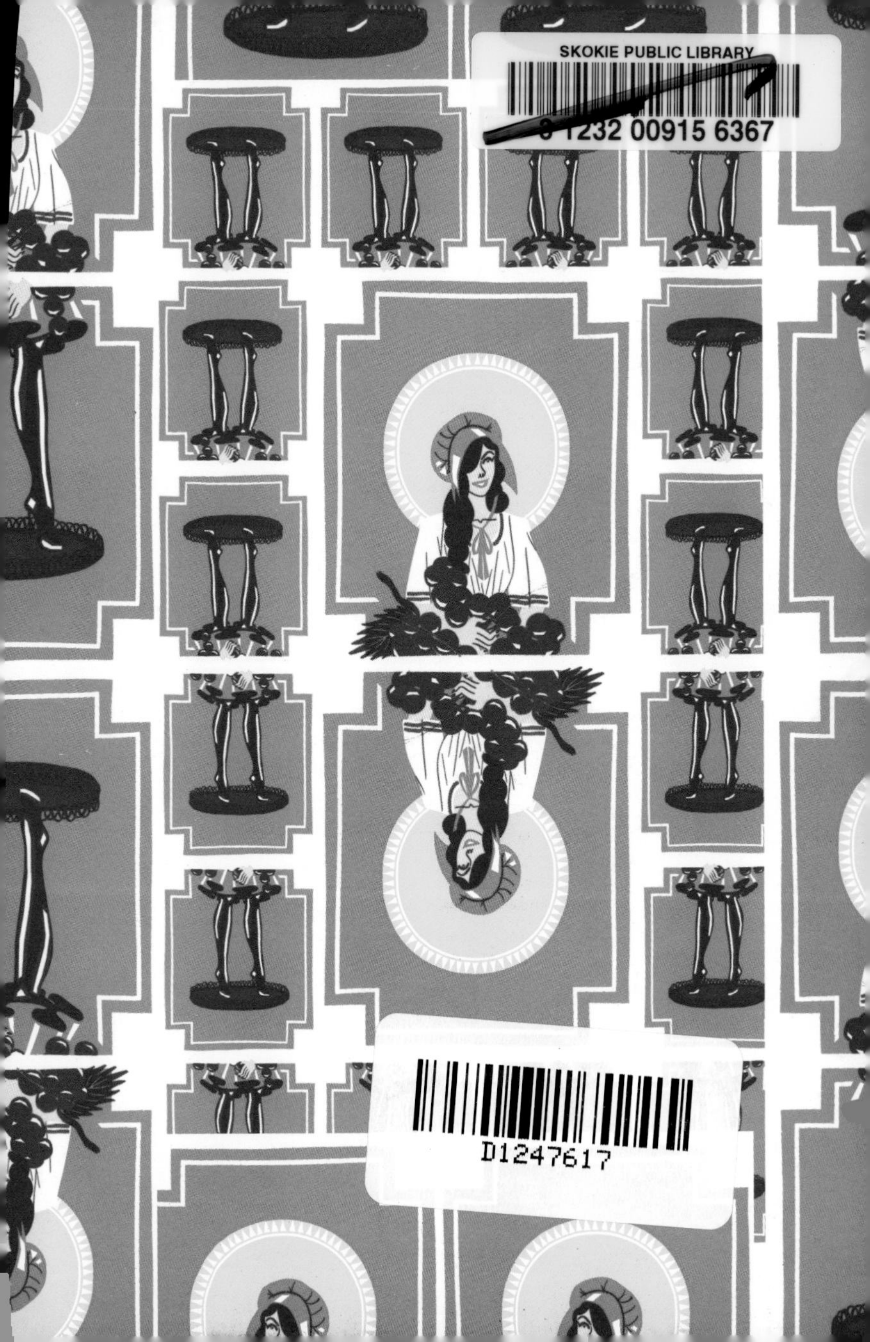

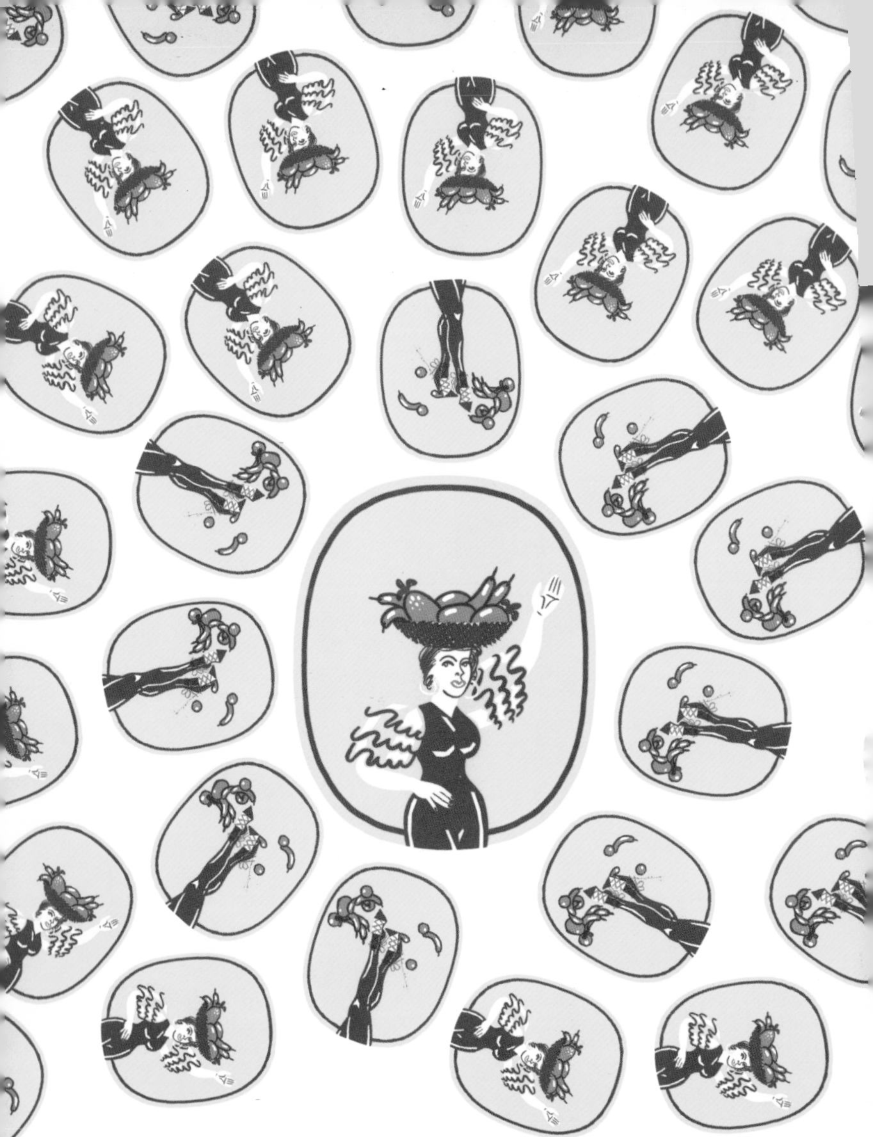

 Published by Koyama Press. koyamapress.com.

First edition: September 2017. Printed in China ISBN: 978-1-927668-47-4

Language Barrier

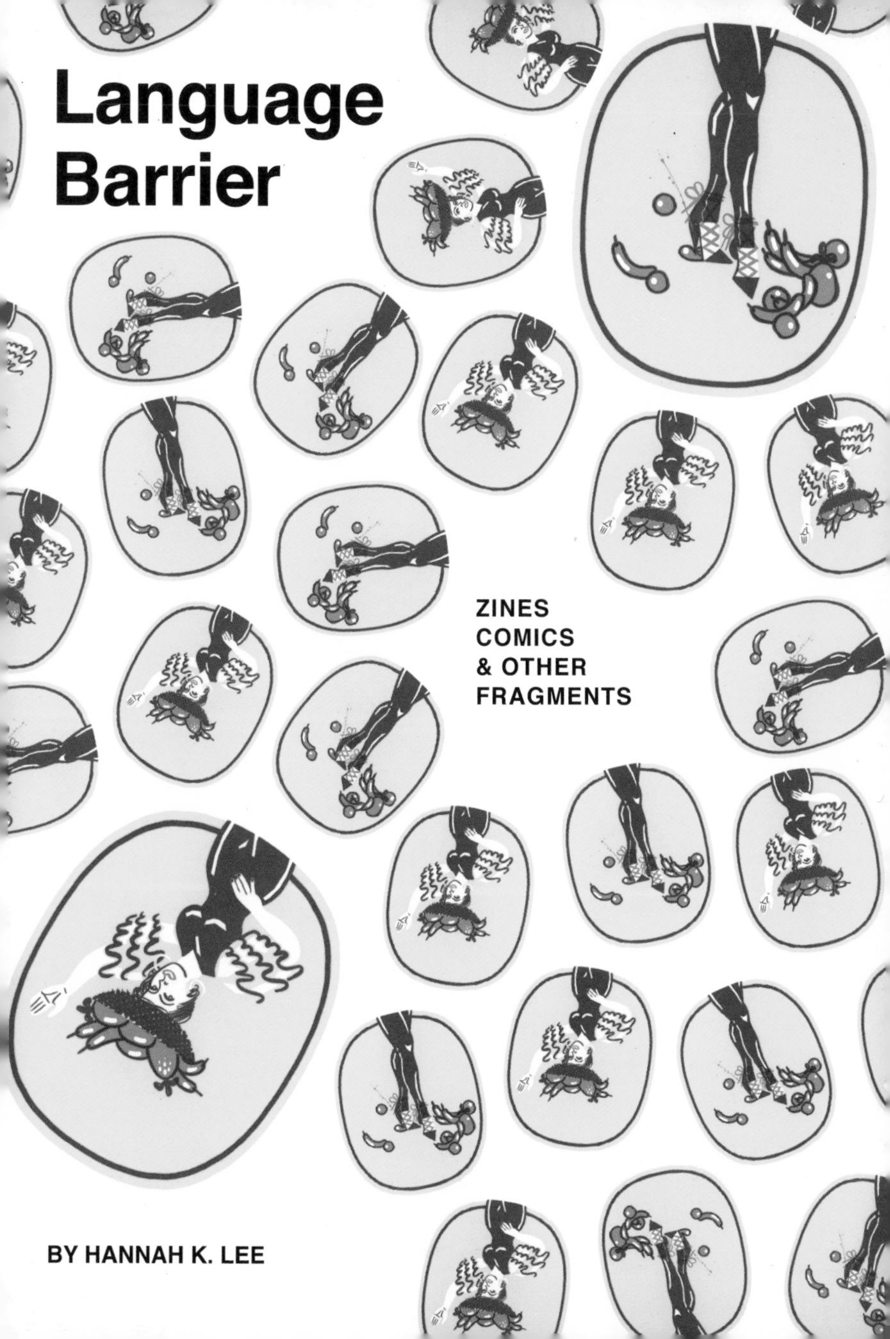

ZINES
COMICS
& OTHER
FRAGMENTS

BY HANNAH K. LEE

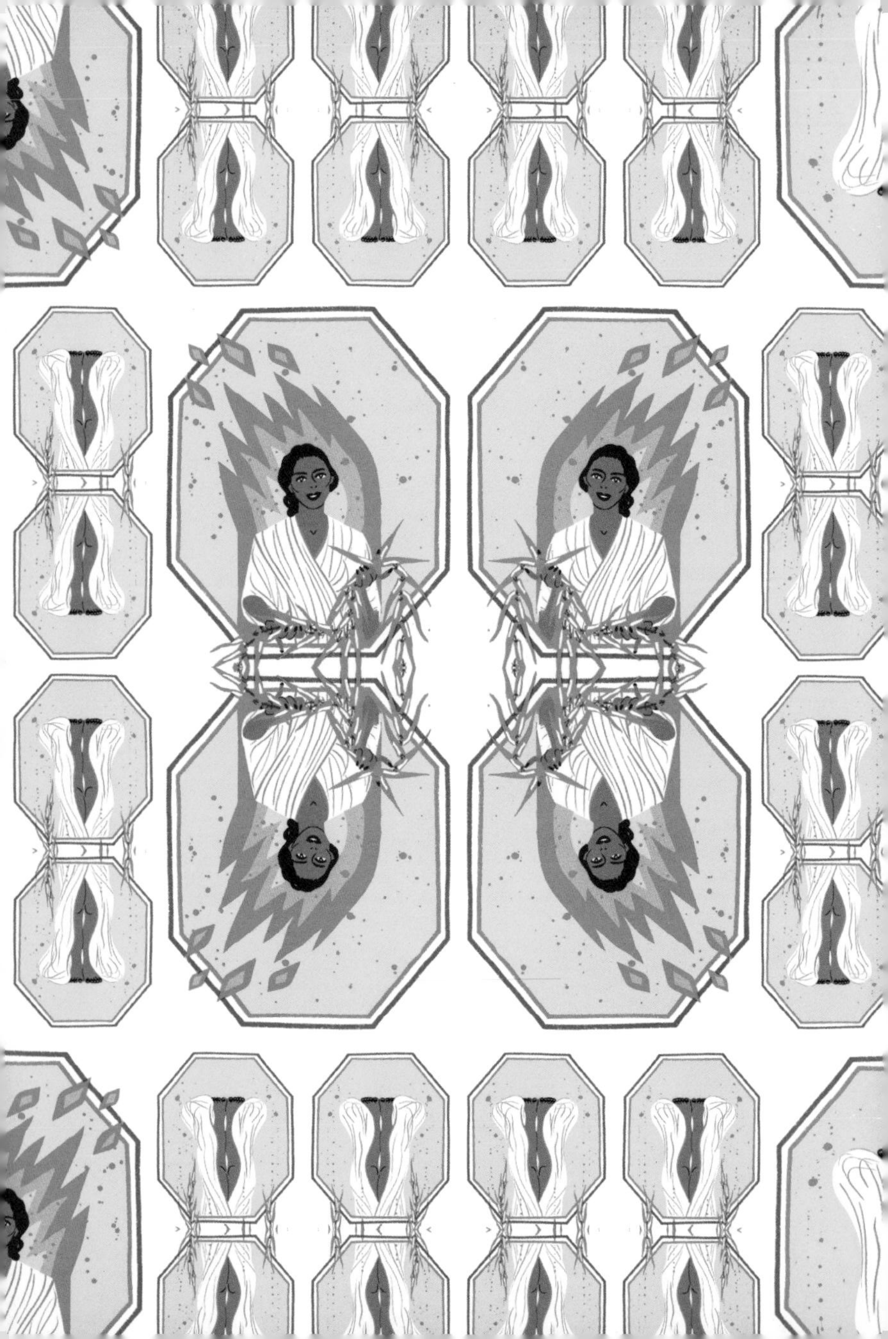

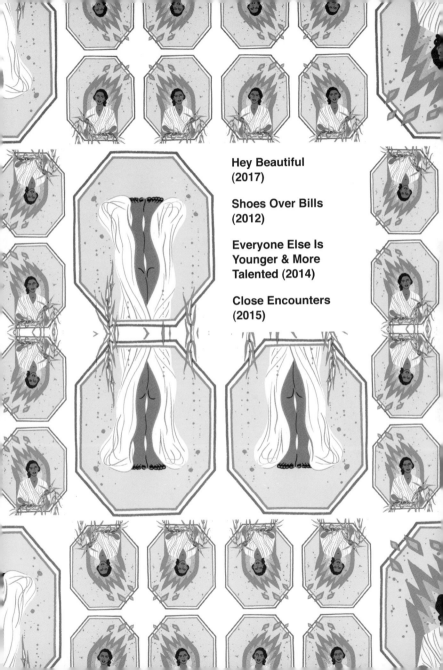

Hey Beautiful
(2017)

Shoes Over Bills
(2012)

Everyone Else Is
Younger & More
Talented (2014)

Close Encounters
(2015)

HEY
BEAU

TIFUL

1 IS THE LONELIEST NUMBER-1

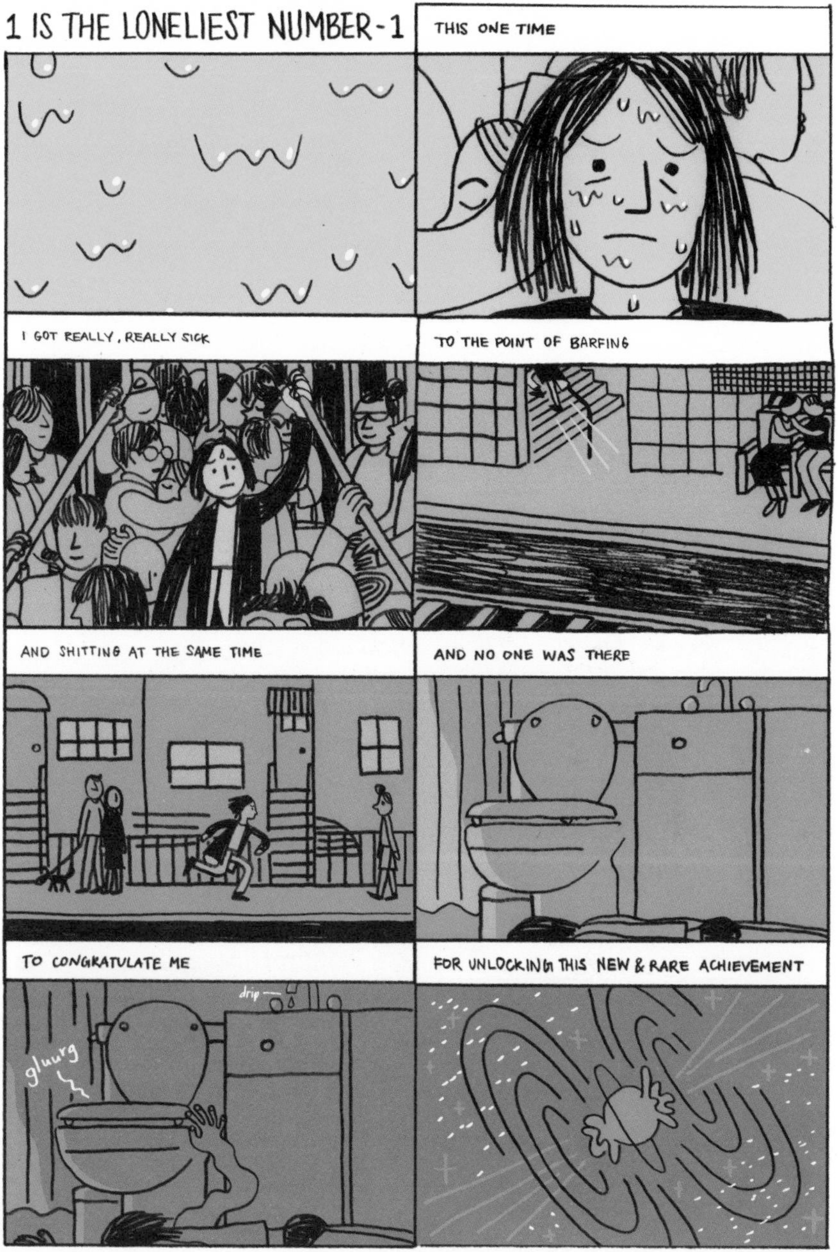
THIS ONE TIME
I GOT REALLY, REALLY SICK
TO THE POINT OF BARFING
AND SHITTING AT THE SAME TIME
AND NO ONE WAS THERE
TO CONGRATULATE ME
FOR UNLOCKING THIS NEW & RARE ACHIEVEMENT
drip
gluurg

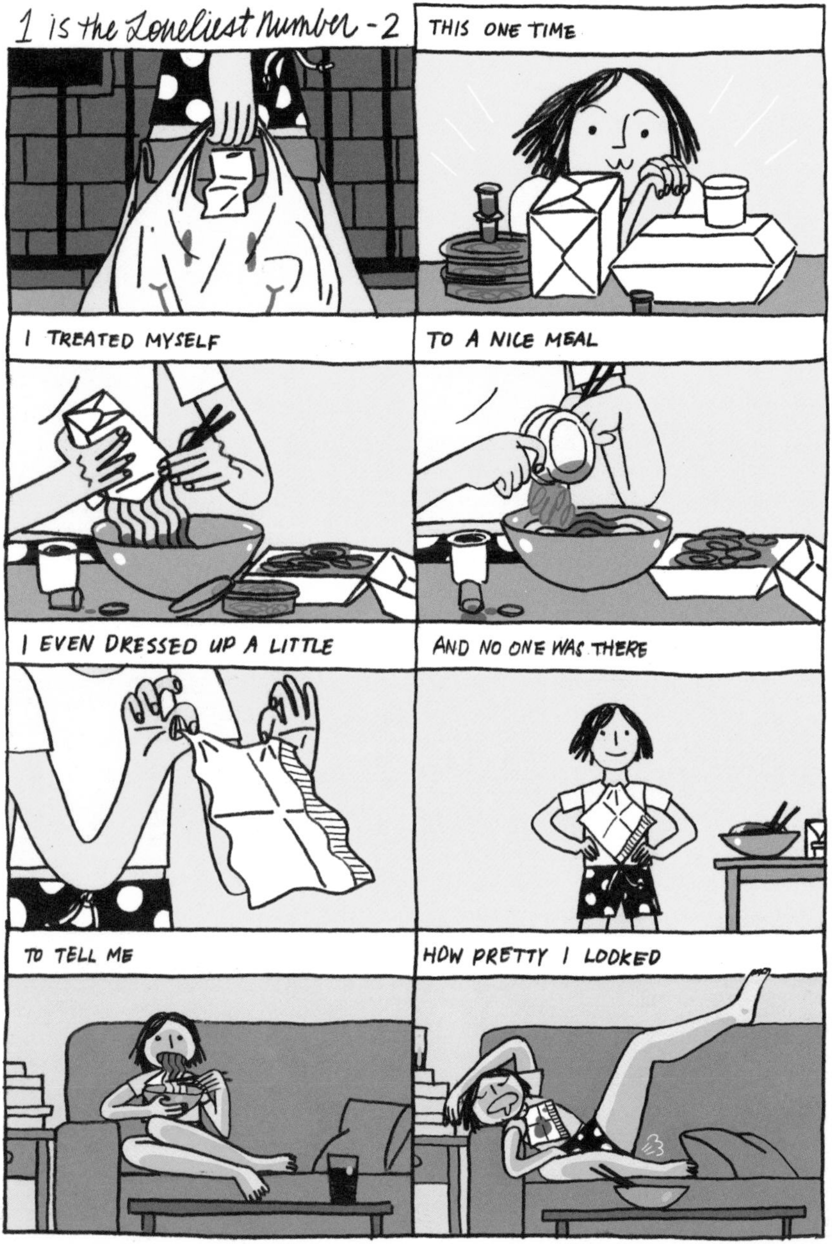
1 is the Loneliest Number - 2
THIS ONE TIME
I TREATED MYSELF
TO A NICE MEAL
I EVEN DRESSED UP A LITTLE
AND NO ONE WAS THERE
TO TELL ME
HOW PRETTY I LOOKED

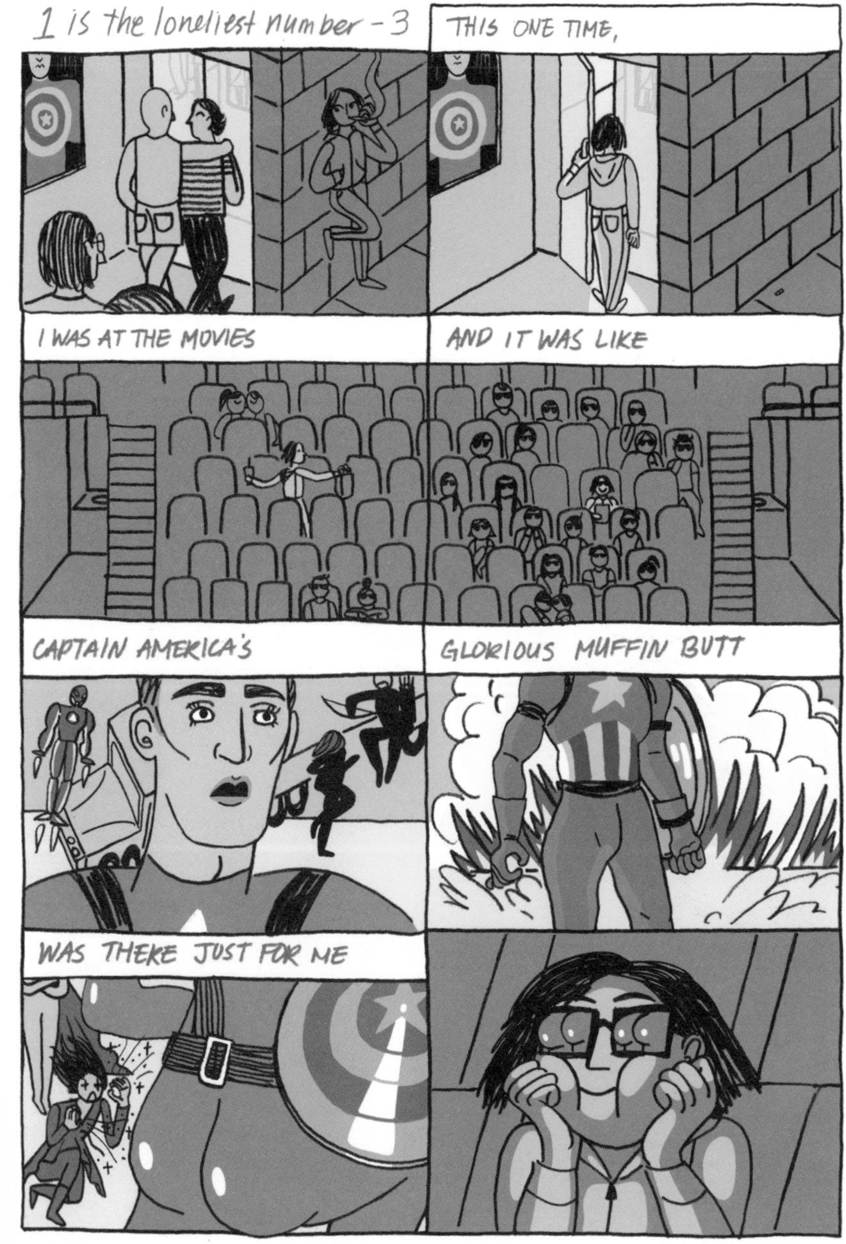
1 is the loneliest number - 3
THIS ONE TIME,
I WAS AT THE MOVIES
AND IT WAS LIKE
CAPTAIN AMERICA'S
GLORIOUS MUFFIN BUTT
WAS THERE JUST FOR ME

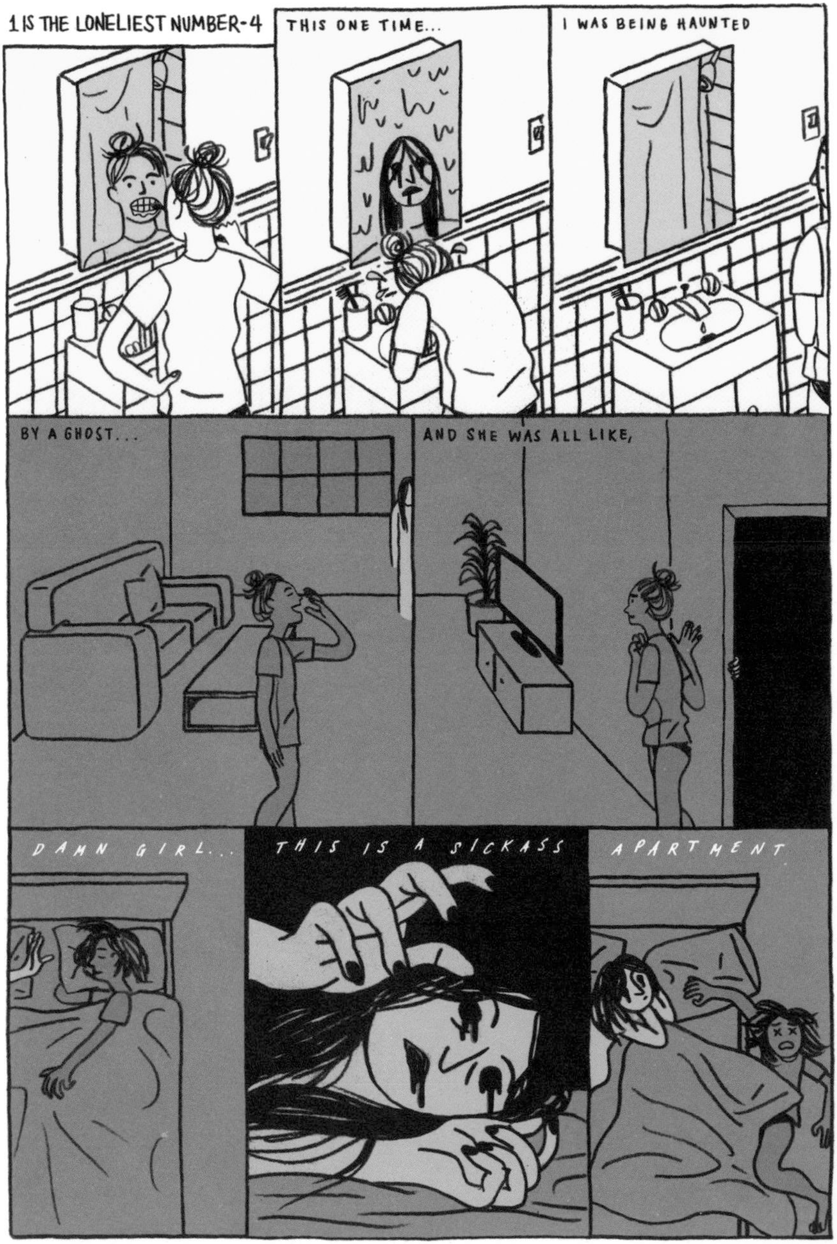
1 IS THE LONELIEST NUMBER-4
THIS ONE TIME...
I WAS BEING HAUNTED
BY A GHOST...
AND SHE WAS ALL LIKE,
DAMN GIRL...
THIS IS A SICKASS
APARTMENT

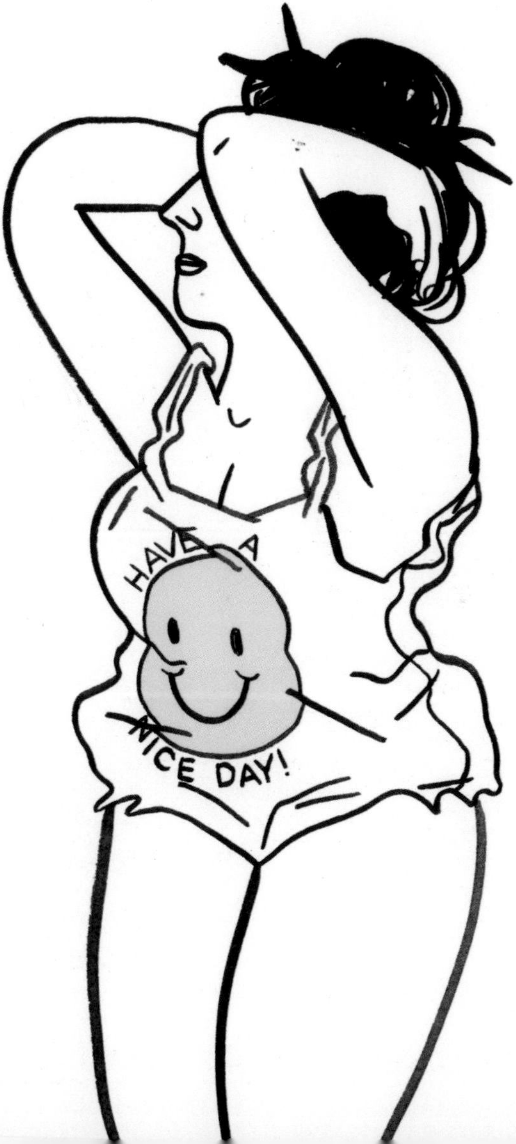
HAVE A
NICE DAY!

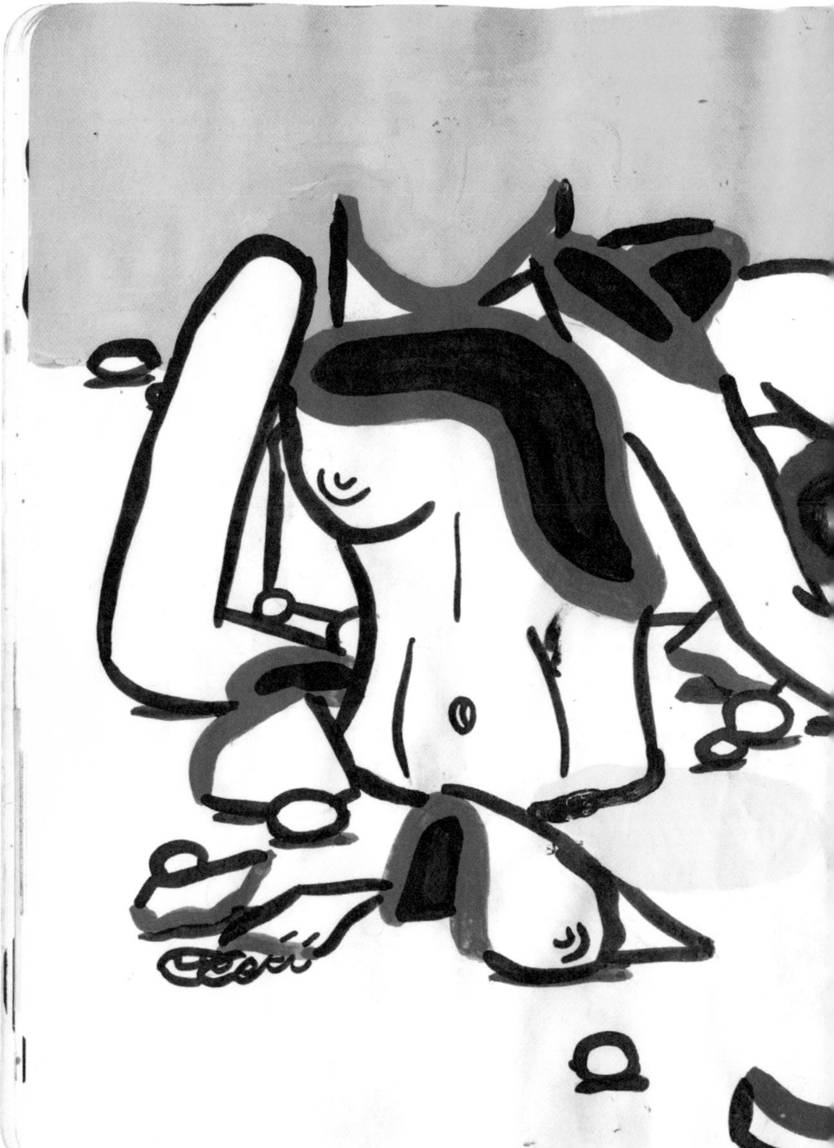

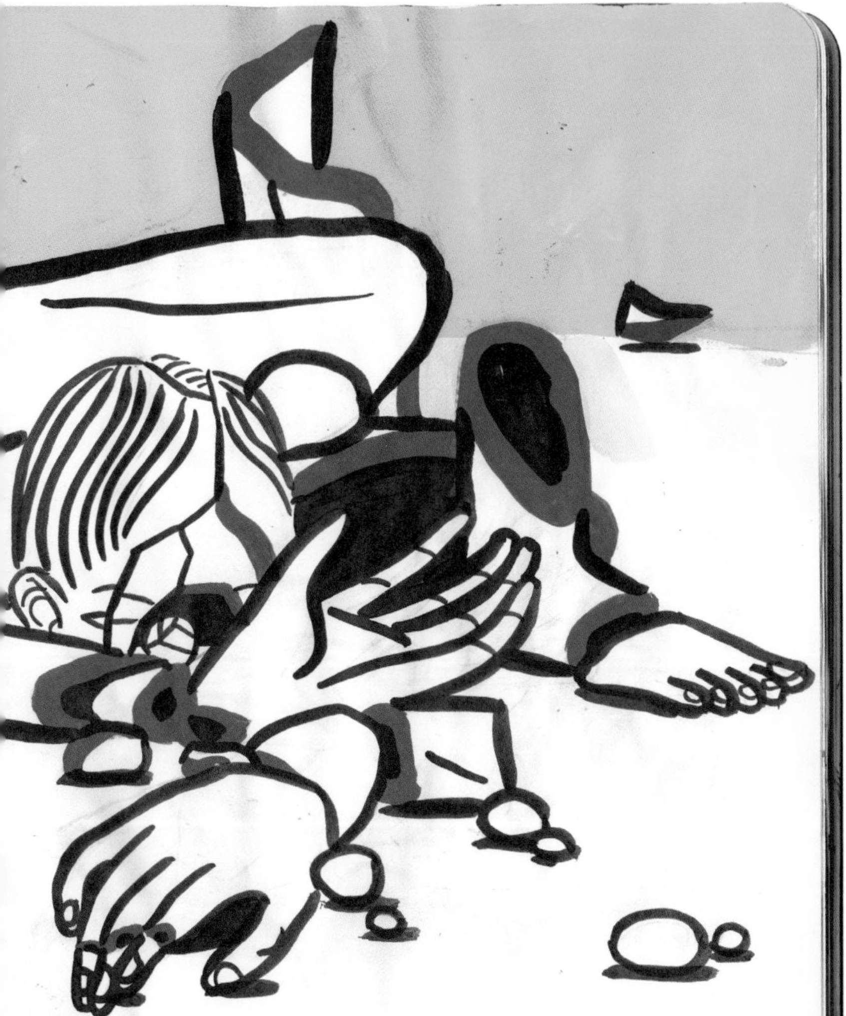

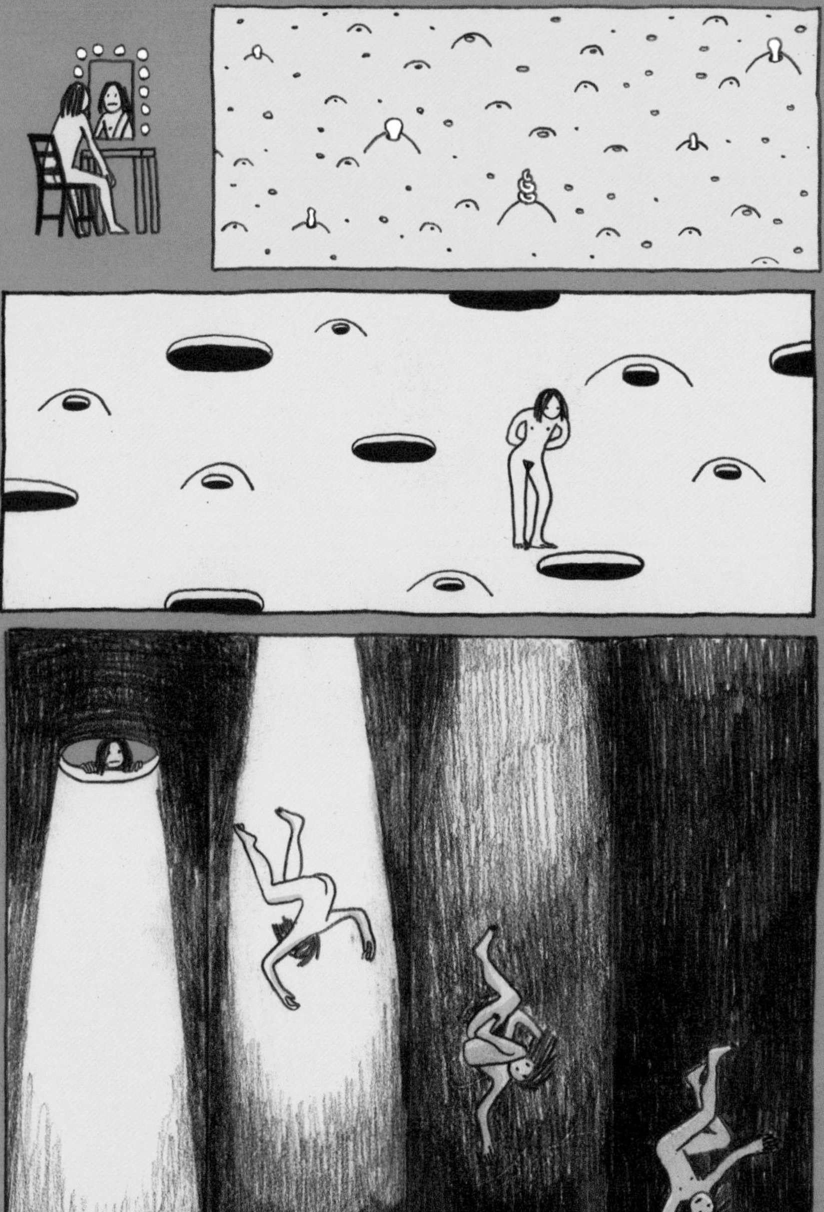

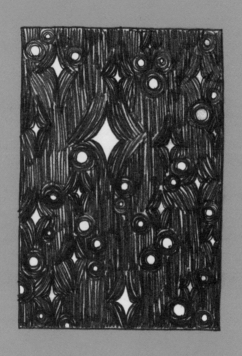

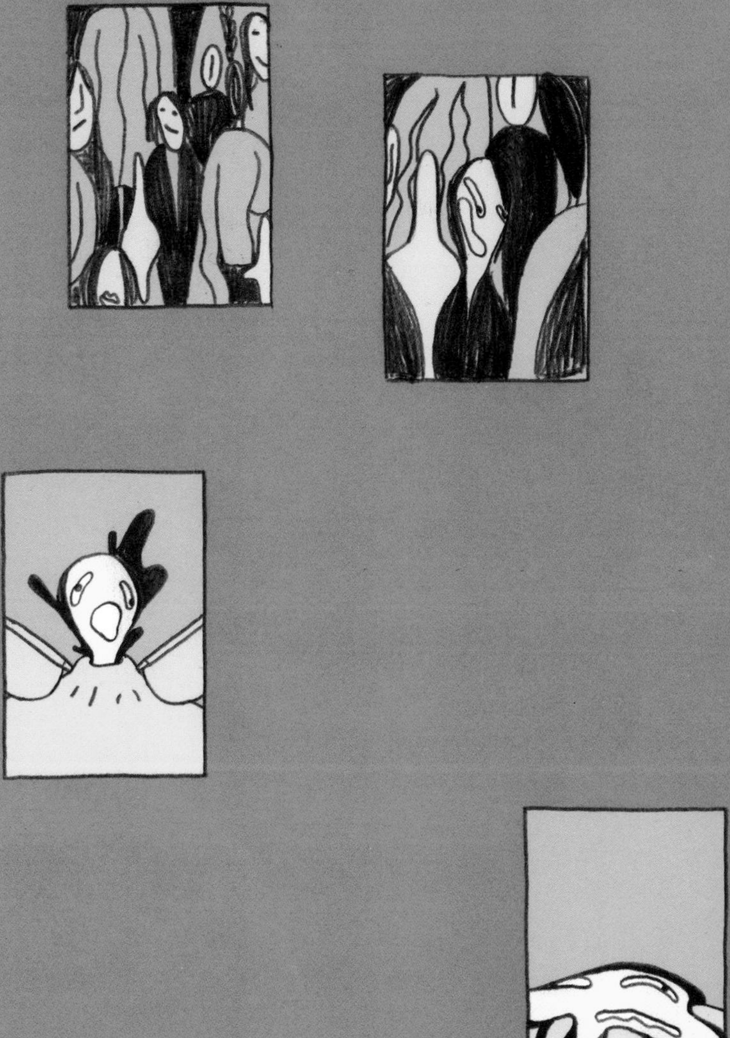

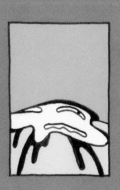

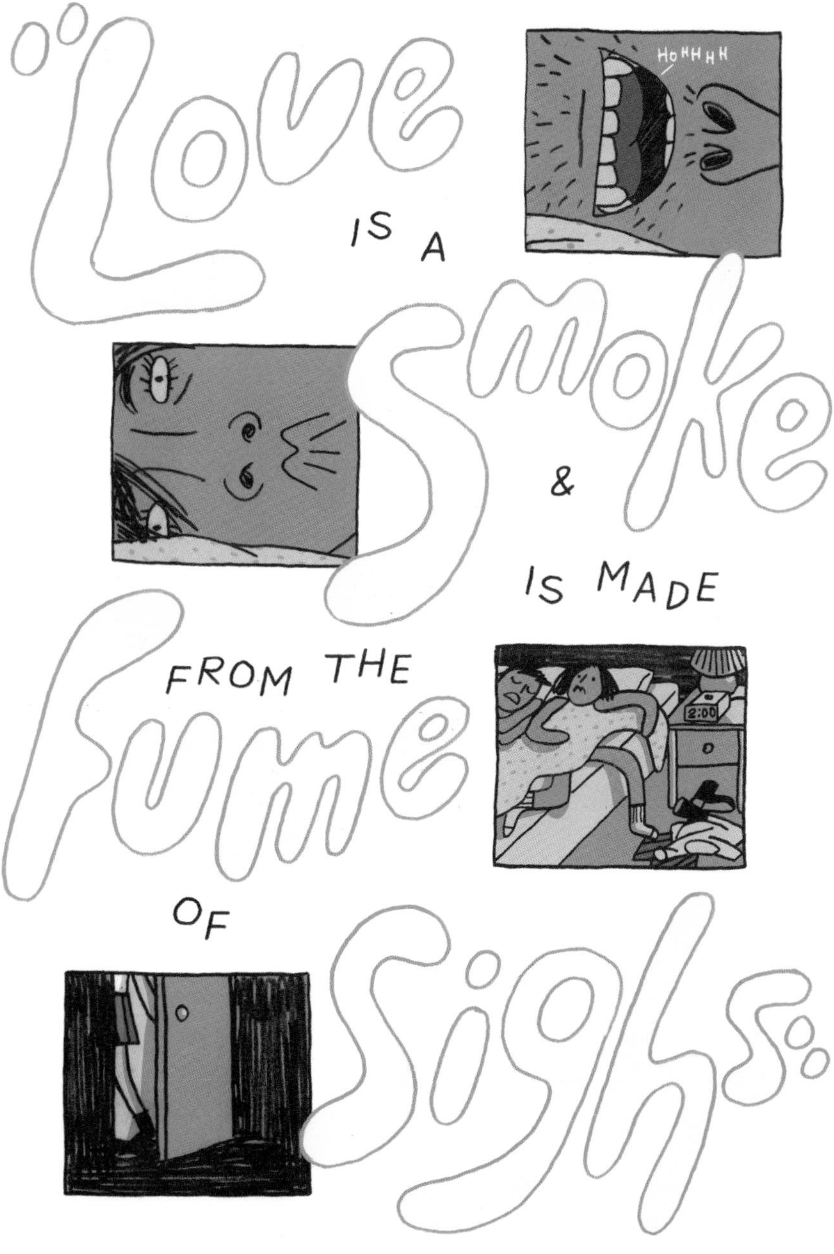
Love
IS A
HOHHHH
Smoke
&
IS MADE
FROM THE
Fume
OF
Sighs.

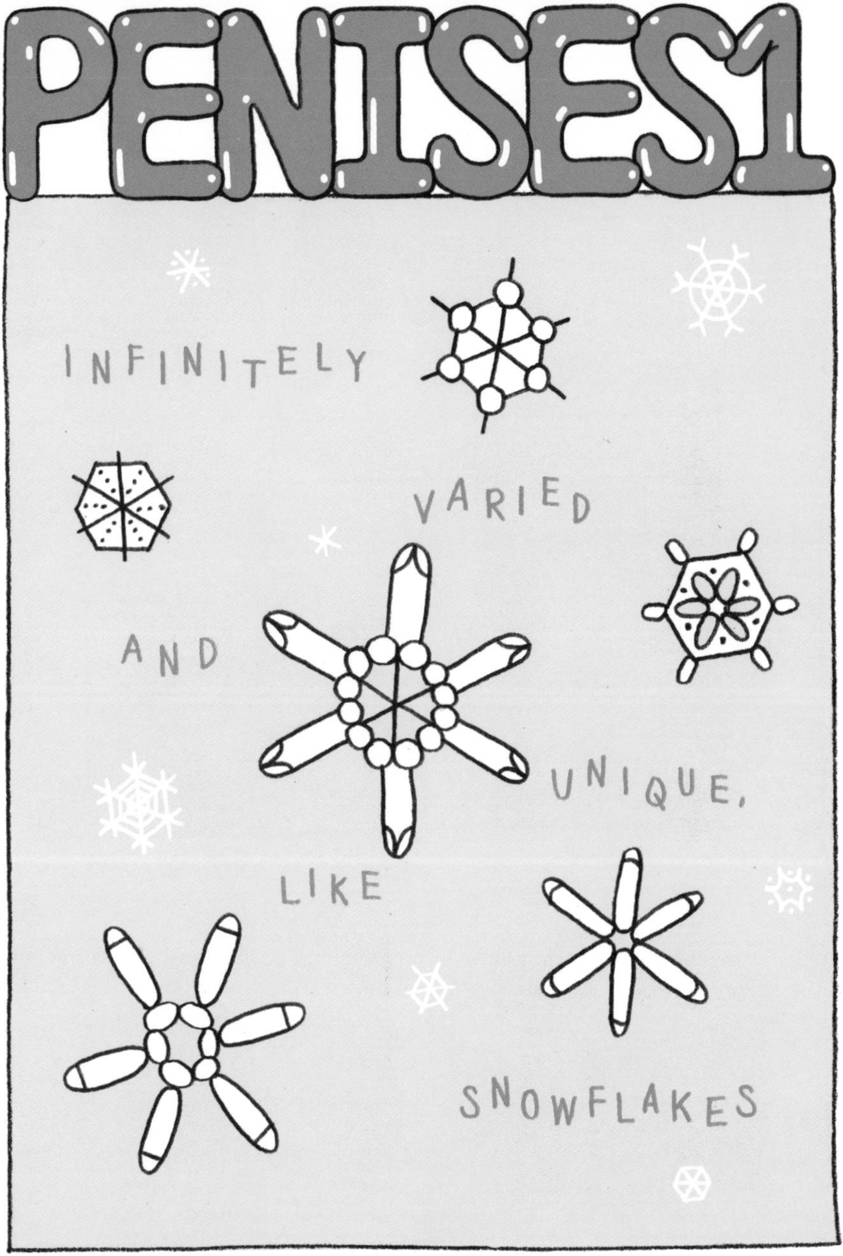
PENISES1
INFINITELY
VARIED
AND
UNIQUE,
LIKE
SNOWFLAKES

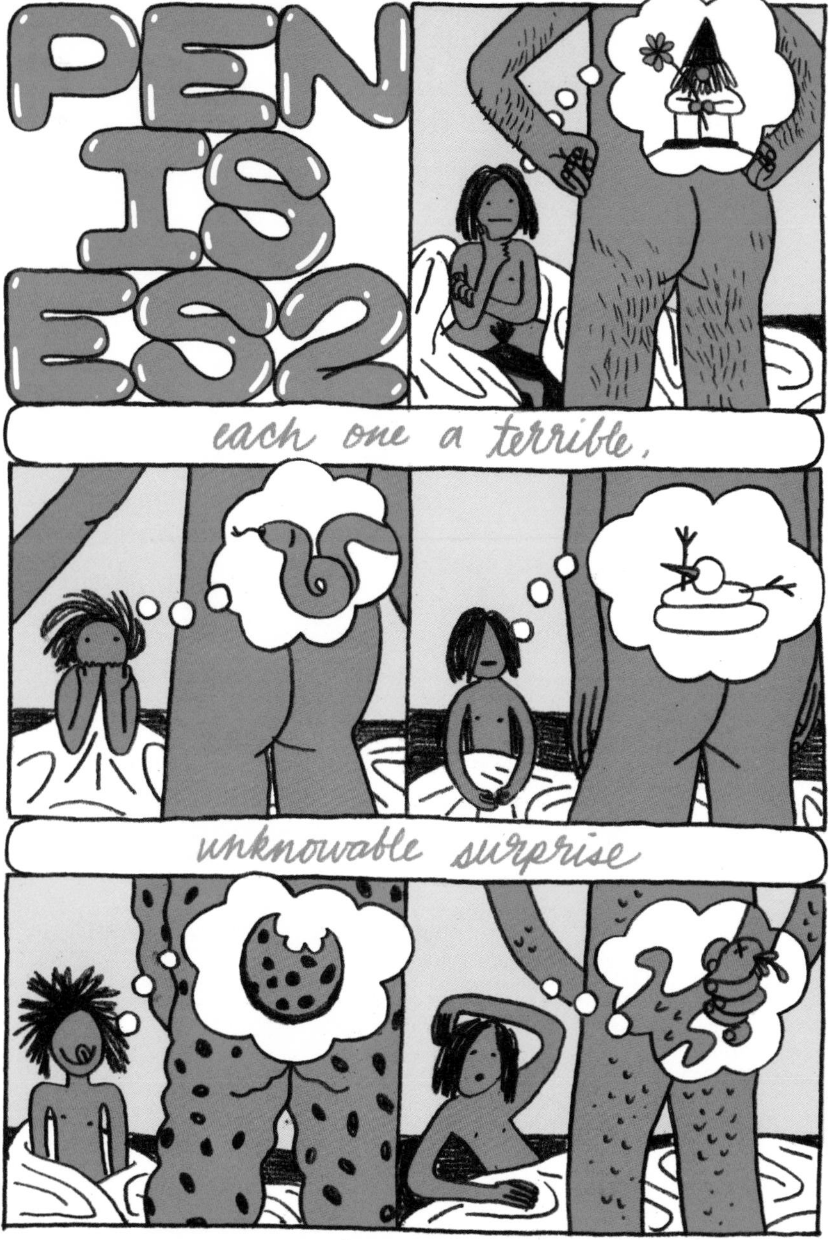
PENISES 2
each one a terrible,
unknowable surprise

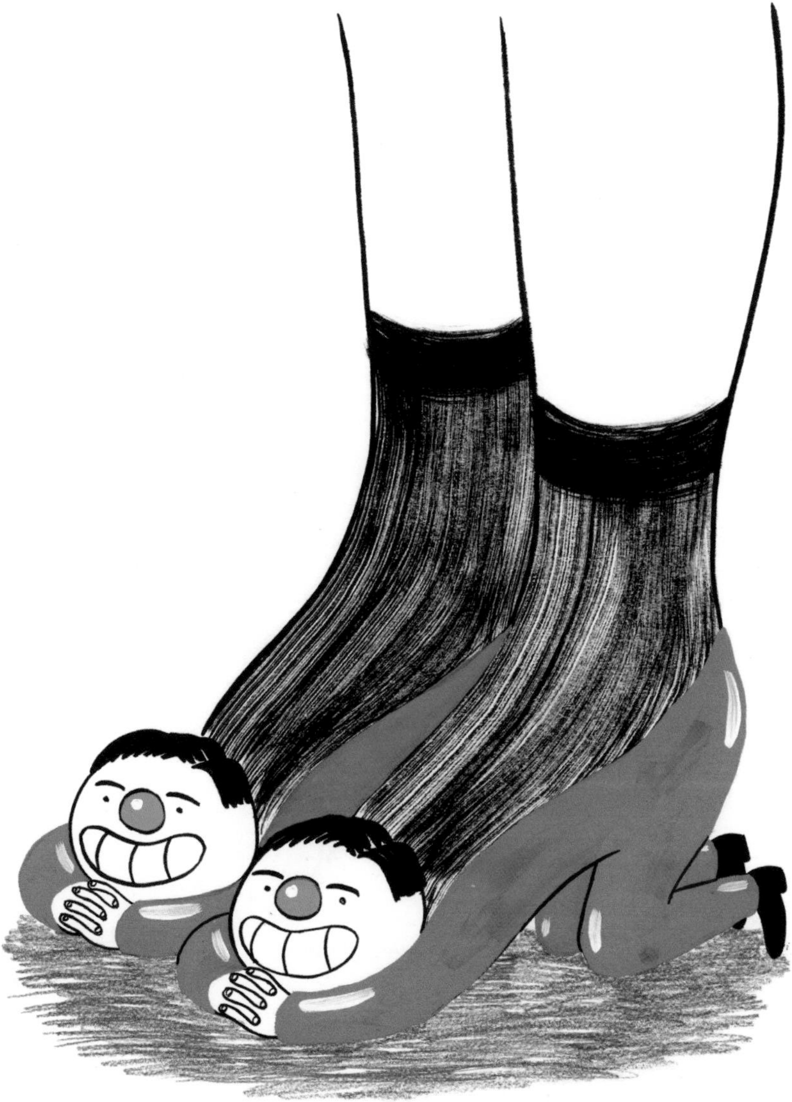

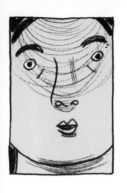

HELLO

'SUP?

HEY BEAUTIFUL

HEY SEXY
HOW ARE YOU?

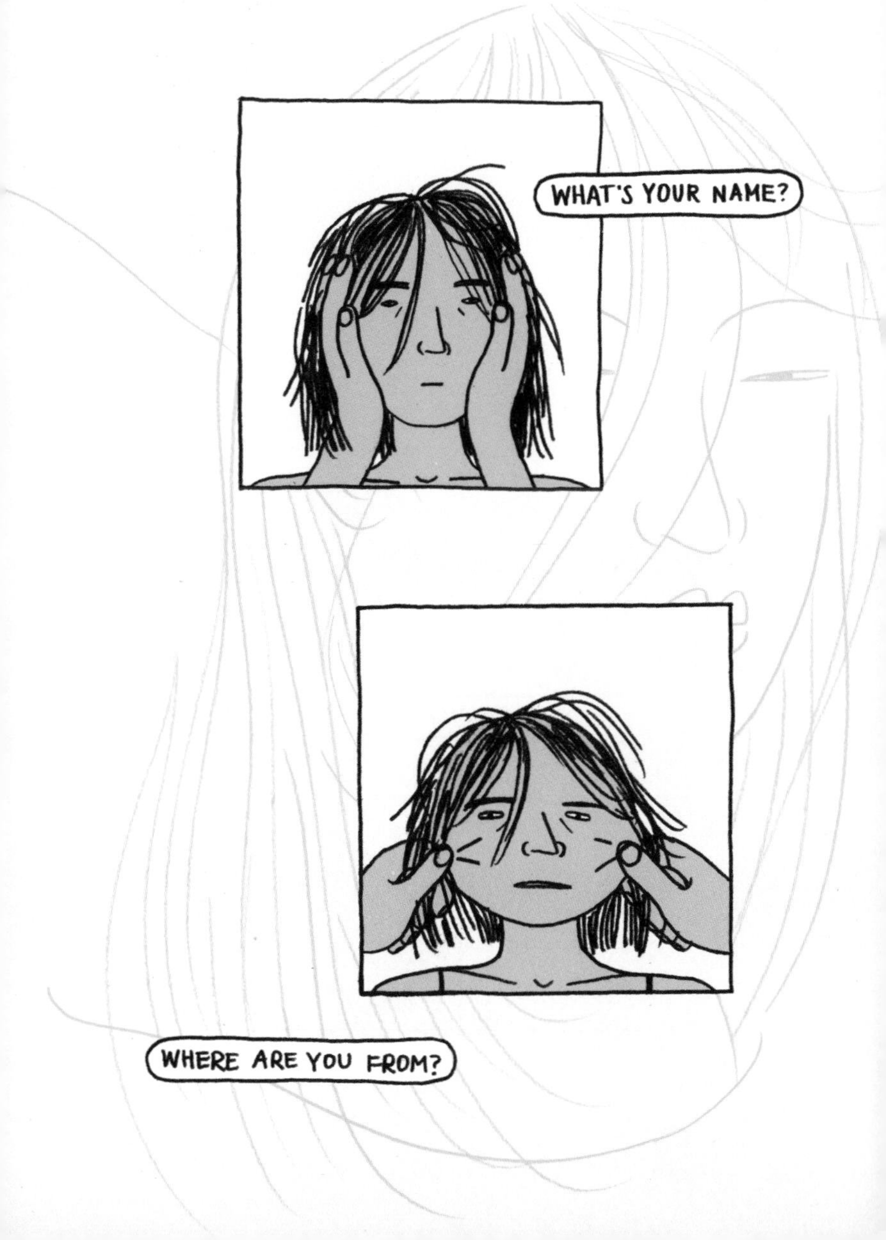
WHAT'S YOUR NAME?
WHERE ARE YOU FROM?

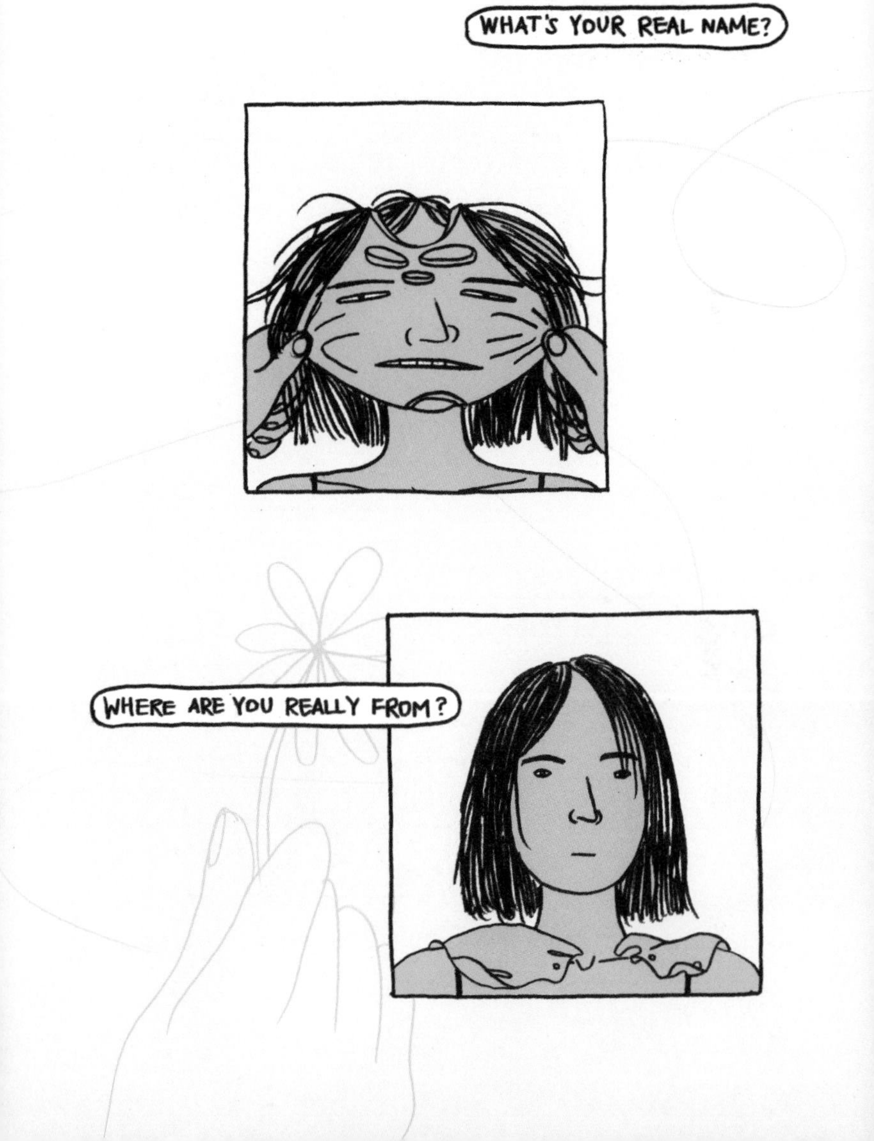
WHAT'S YOUR REAL NAME?
WHERE ARE YOU REALLY FROM?

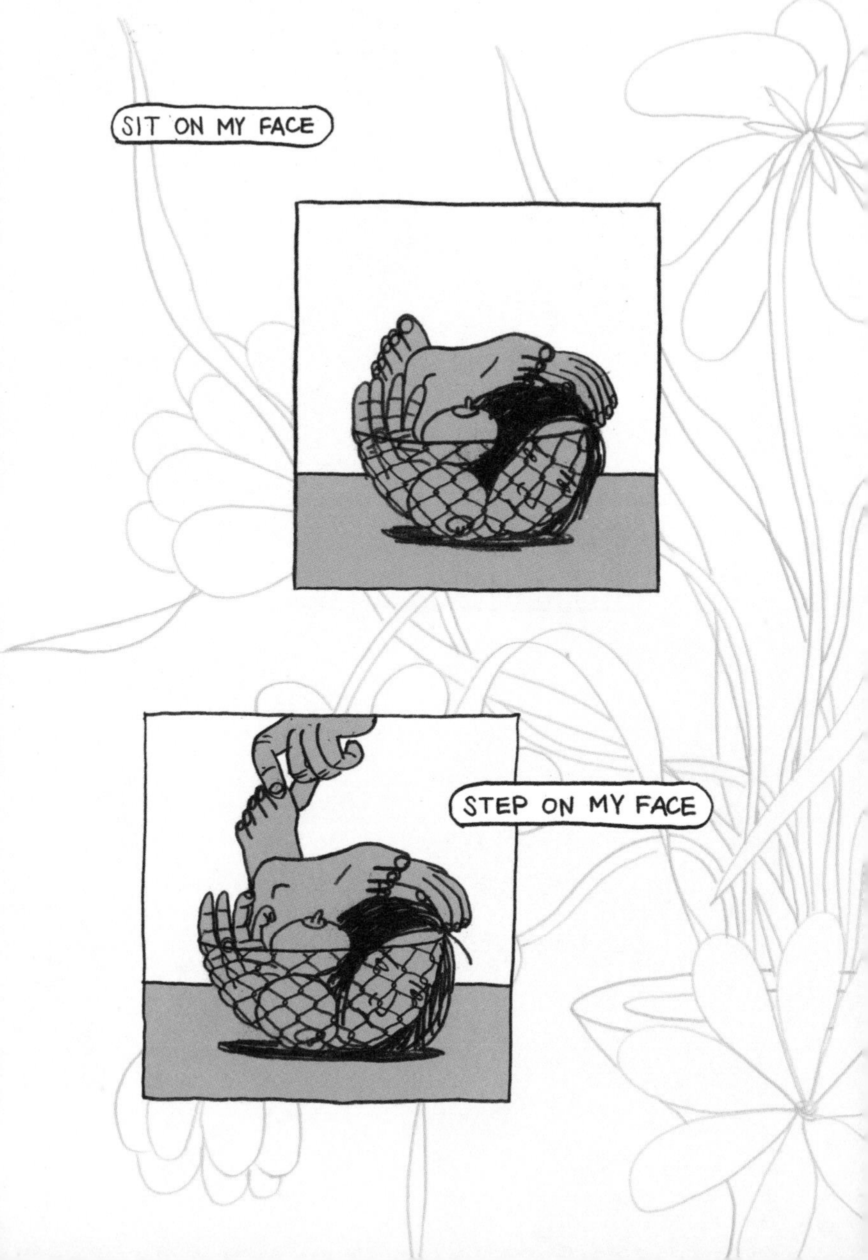
SIT ON MY FACE
STEP ON MY FACE

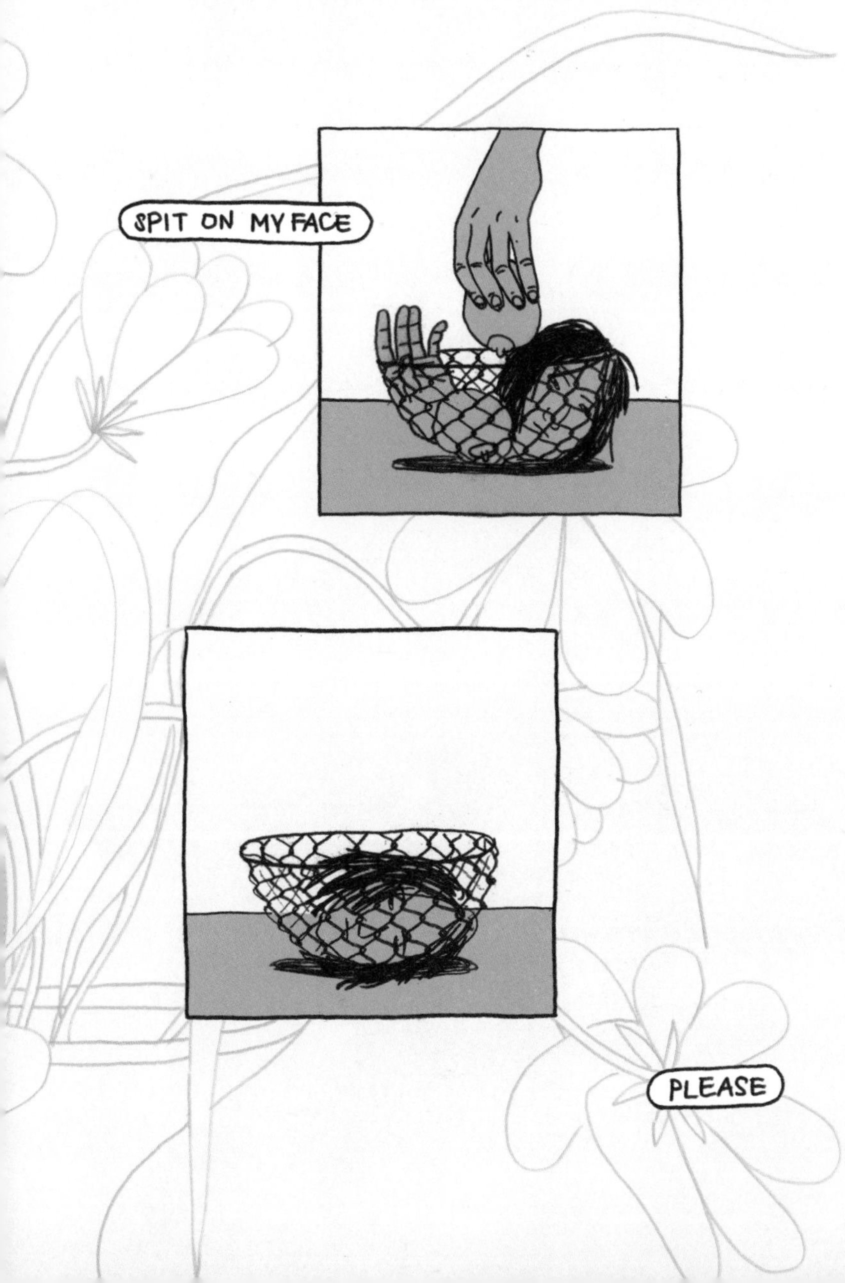
SPIT ON MY FACE
PLEASE

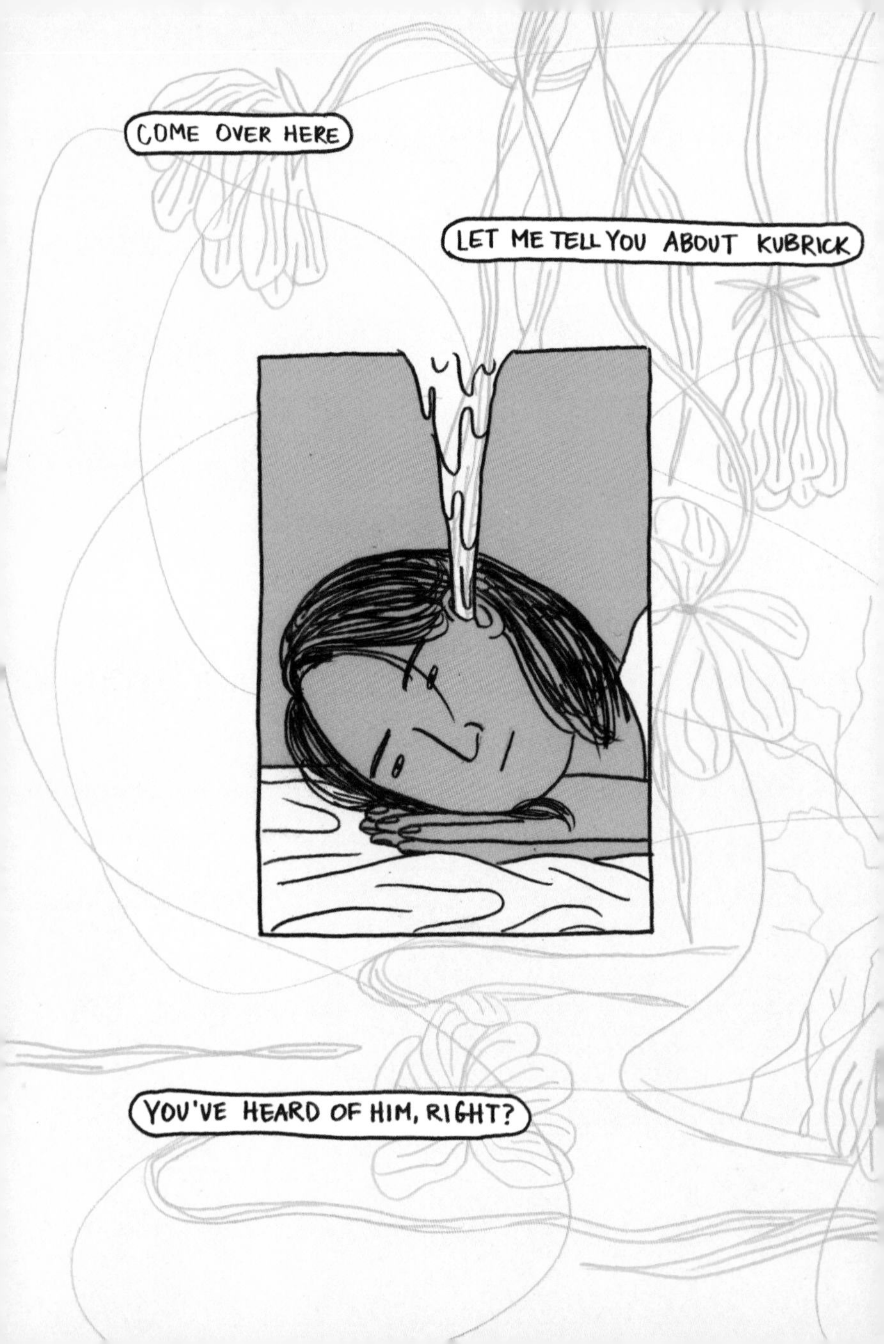
COME OVER HERE
LET ME TELL YOU ABOUT KUBRICK
YOU'VE HEARD OF HIM, RIGHT?

LET ME TELL YOU ABOUT RADIOHEAD

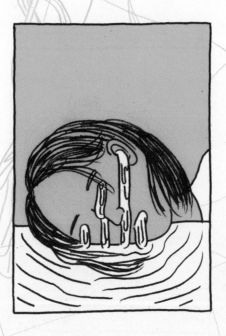

LET ME TELL YOU ABOUT BATTLESTAR GALACTICA

(THE ORIGINAL)

I BET YOU'RE A GOOD GIRL

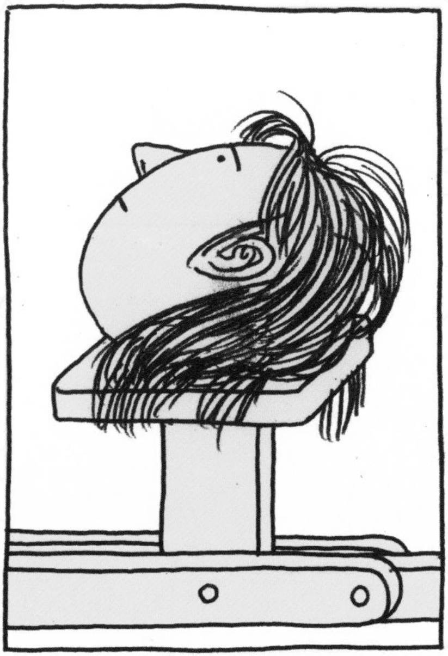

I BET YOU'RE A TOTAL PRUDE

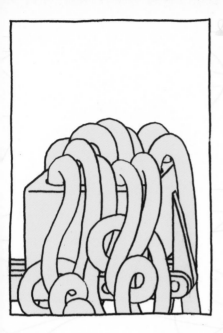

I BET YOU'RE A BAD GIRL

I BET YOU LIKE IT ROUGH

HOT PICS

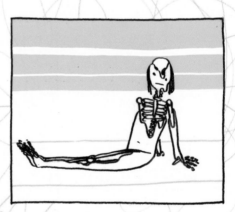

I BET I COULD GET YOU

TO SMILE

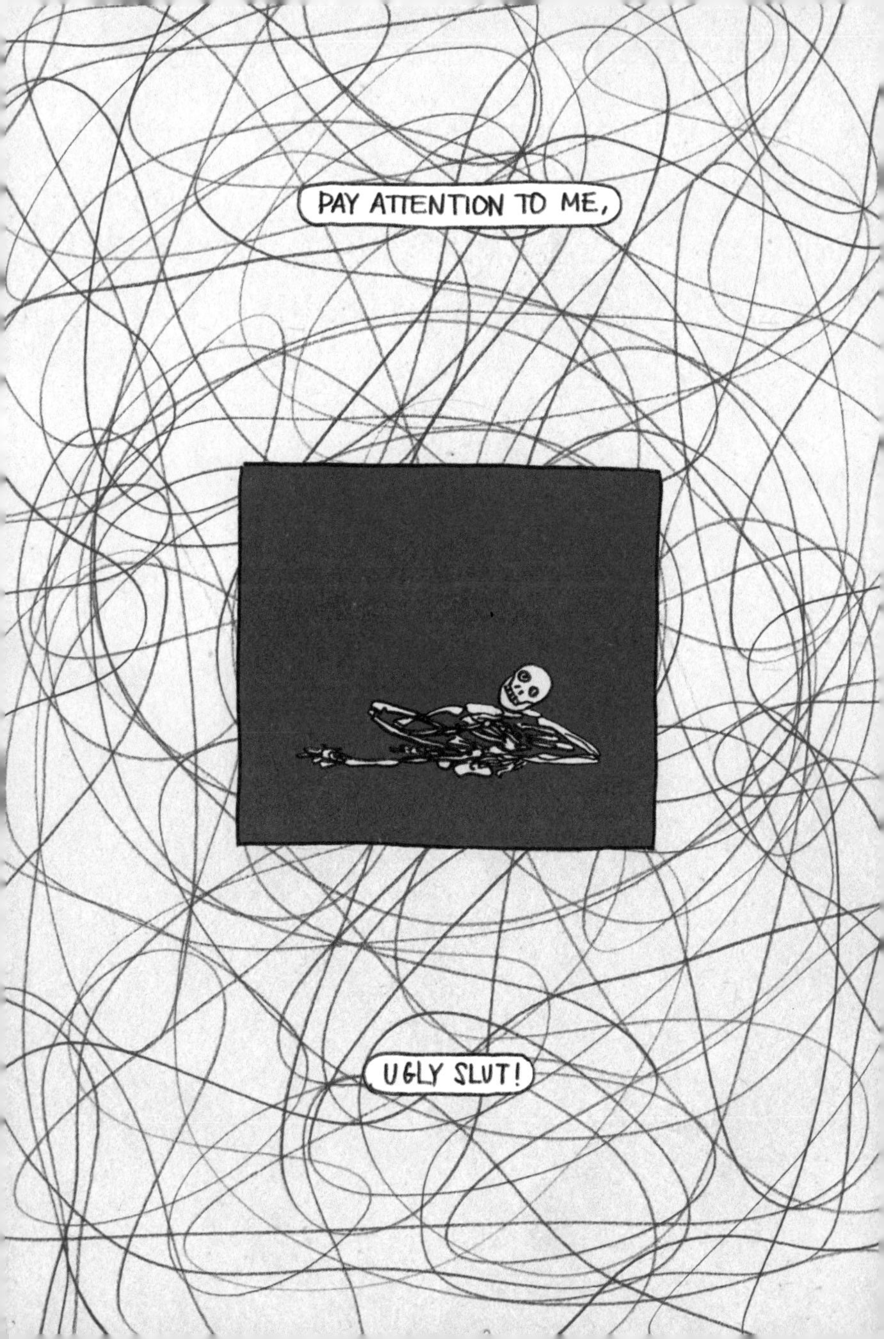
PAY ATTENTION TO ME,
UGLY SLUT!

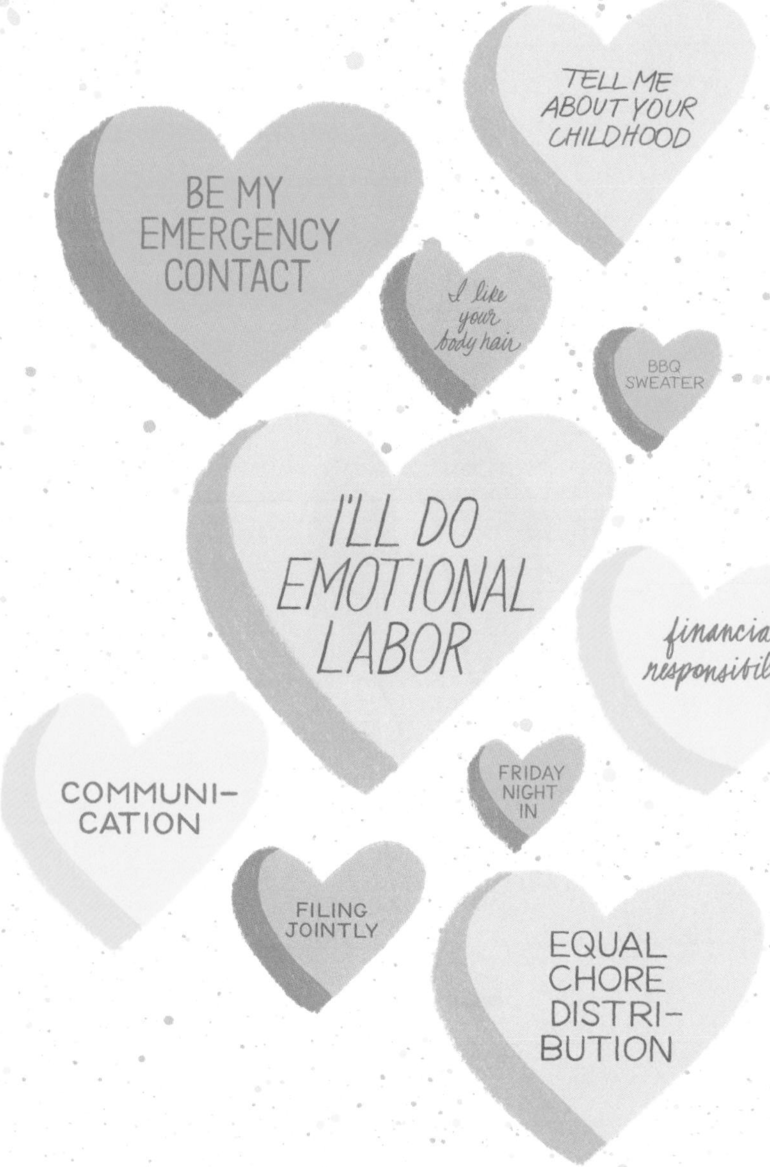
TELL ME ABOUT YOUR CHILDHOOD
BE MY EMERGENCY CONTACT
I like your body hair
BBQ SWEATER
I'LL DO EMOTIONAL LABOR
financial responsibility
COMMUNI-CATION
FRIDAY NIGHT IN
FILING JOINTLY
EQUAL CHORE DISTRI-BUTION

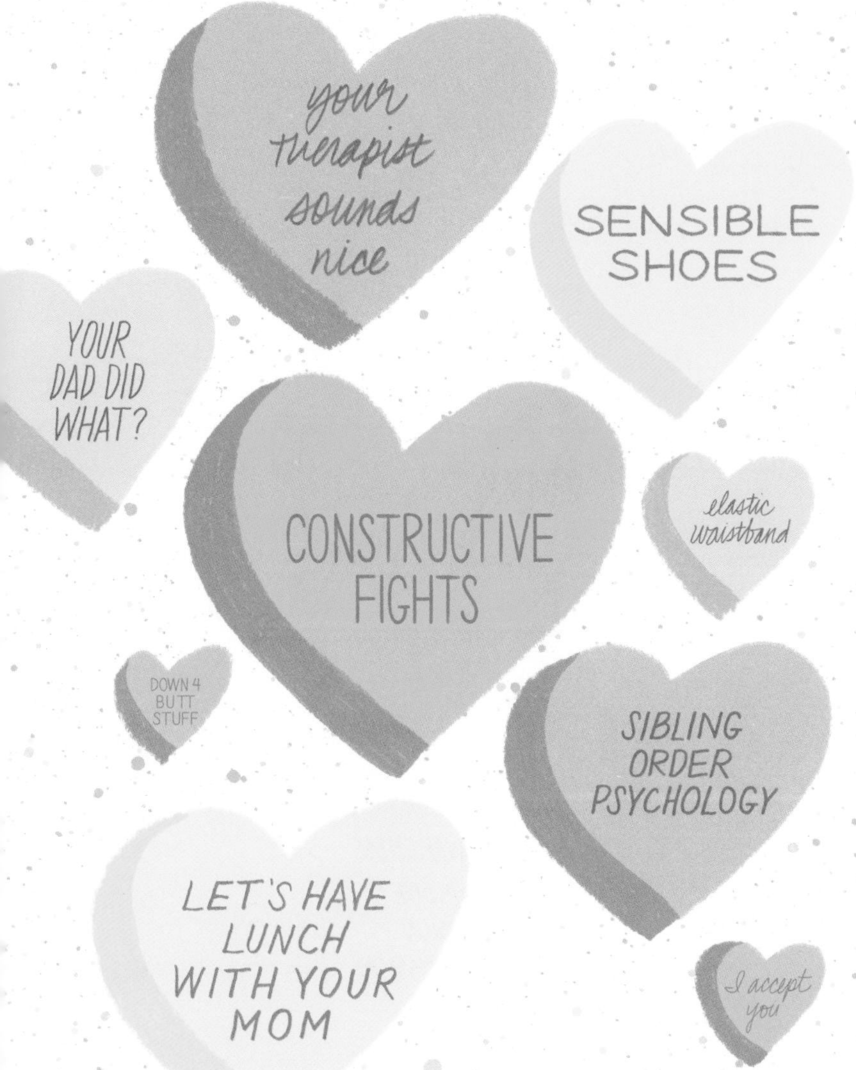
your therapist sounds nice
SENSIBLE SHOES
YOUR DAD DID WHAT?
CONSTRUCTIVE FIGHTS
elastic waistband
DOWN 4 BUTT STUFF
SIBLING ORDER PSYCHOLOGY
LET'S HAVE LUNCH WITH YOUR MOM
I accept you

AWARENESS
OF ONE'S
OWN
NARCISSISM

INTERPRETING EMOJI SEXTS

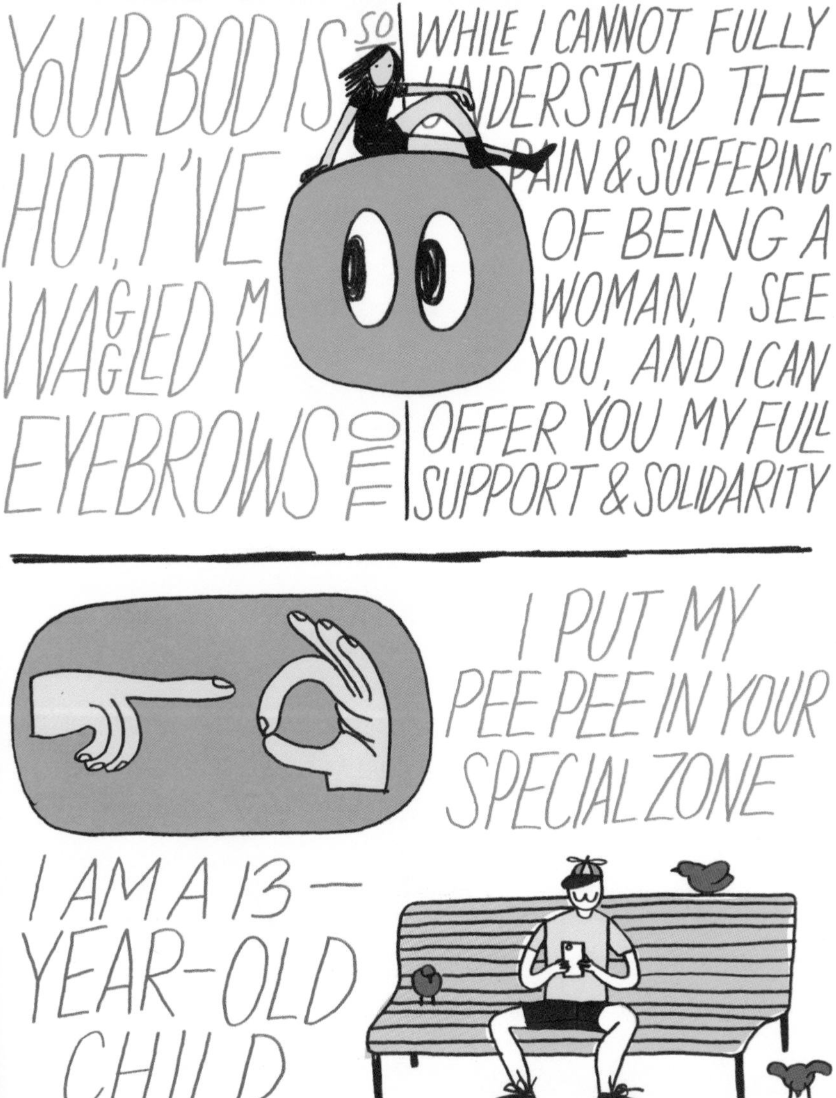
YOUR BOD IS SO HOT I'VE WAGGLED MY EYEBROWS OFF
WHILE I CANNOT FULLY UNDERSTAND THE PAIN & SUFFERING OF BEING A WOMAN, I SEE YOU, AND I CAN OFFER YOU MY FULL SUPPORT & SOLIDARITY
I PUT MY PEE PEE IN YOUR SPECIAL ZONE
I AM A 13-YEAR-OLD CHILD

HEY STRANGER,
HOW 'BOUT
WE SNORT
SOME COKE

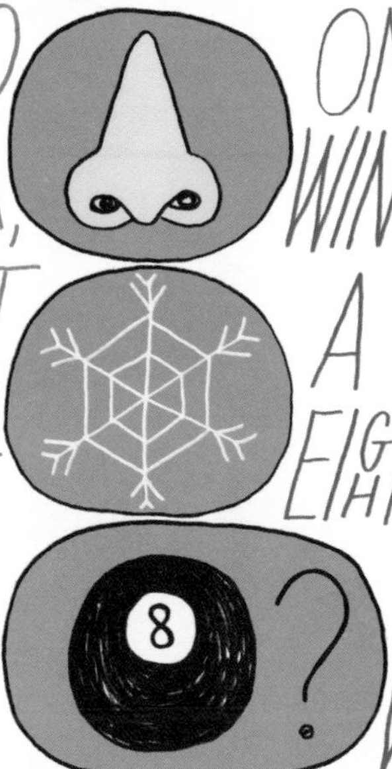

ON A COLD
WINTER'S NIGHT,
A MAGIC
EIGHT BALL TOLD
ME THAT I
WILL DIE ALONE

CUNNILINGUS &
SEX AVEC MOI?

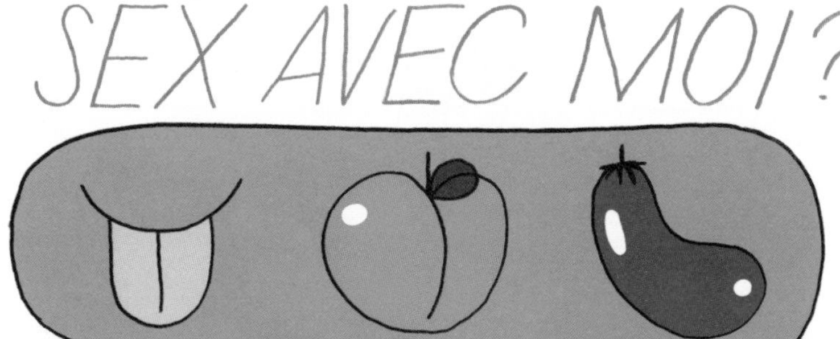

I AM CONCERNED ABOUT THE
FOLATE CONTENT OF YOUR DIET

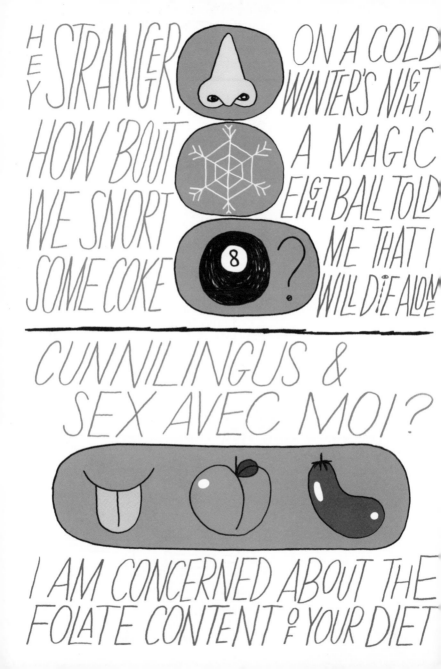

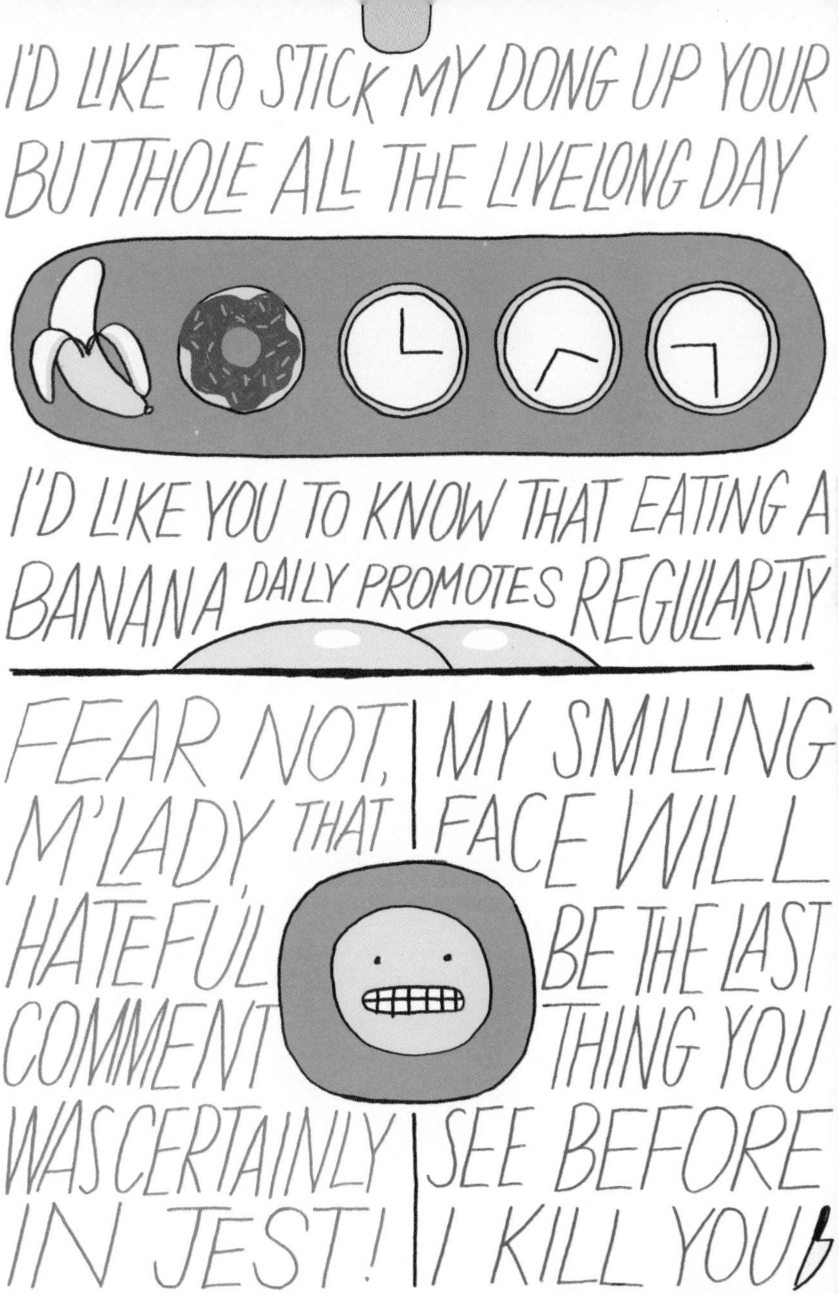
I'D LIKE TO STICK MY DONG UP YOUR BUTTHOLE ALL THE LIVELONG DAY
I'D LIKE YOU TO KNOW THAT EATING A BANANA DAILY PROMOTES REGULARITY
FEAR NOT, M'LADY, THAT HATEFUL COMMENT WAS CERTAINLY IN JEST!
MY SMILING FACE WILL BE THE LAST THING YOU SEE BEFORE I KILL YOU

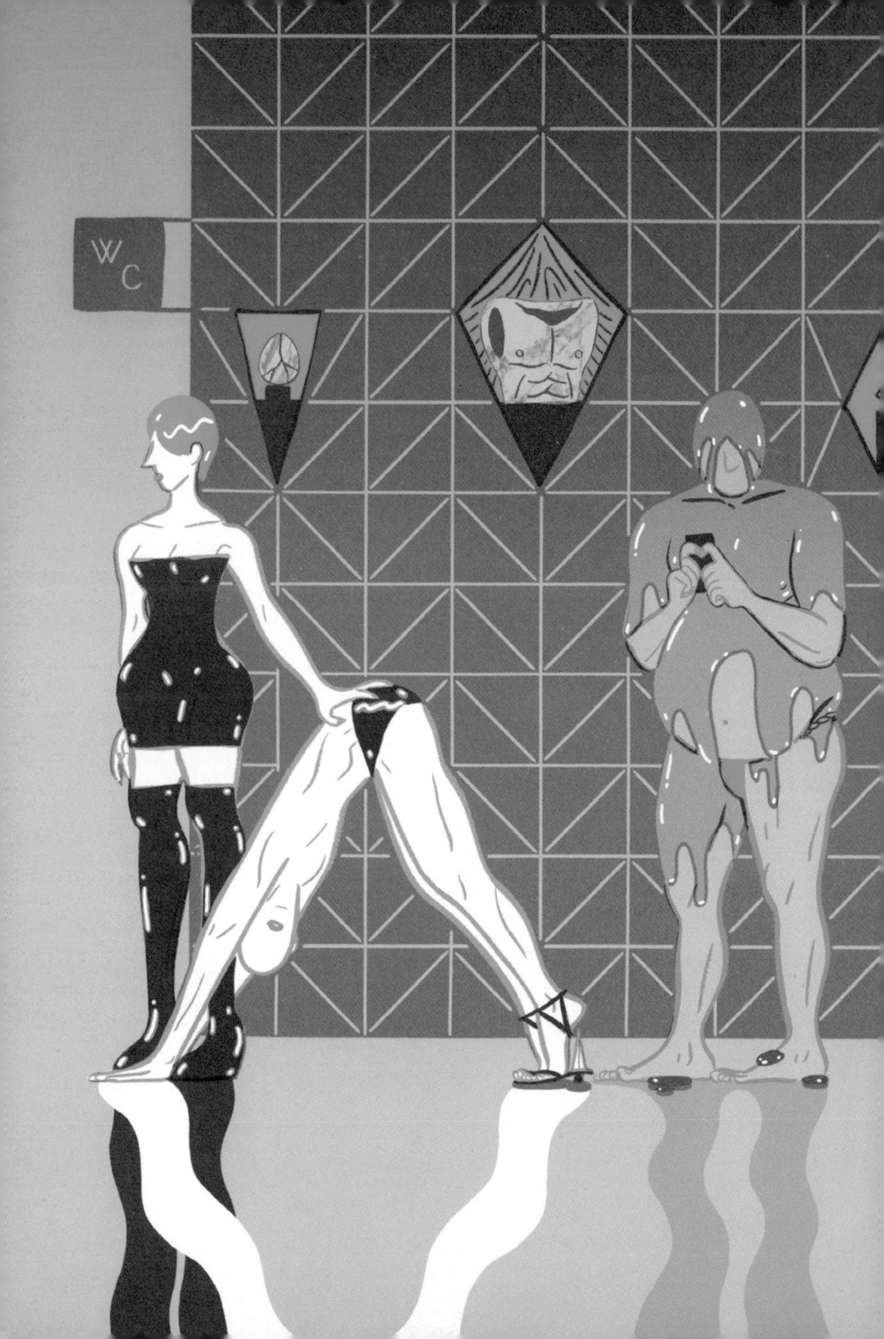
WC

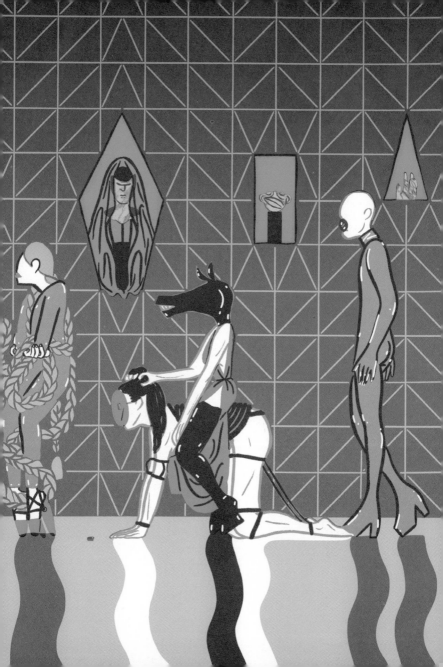

ISSUES#2

SHOES OVER BILLS

$10

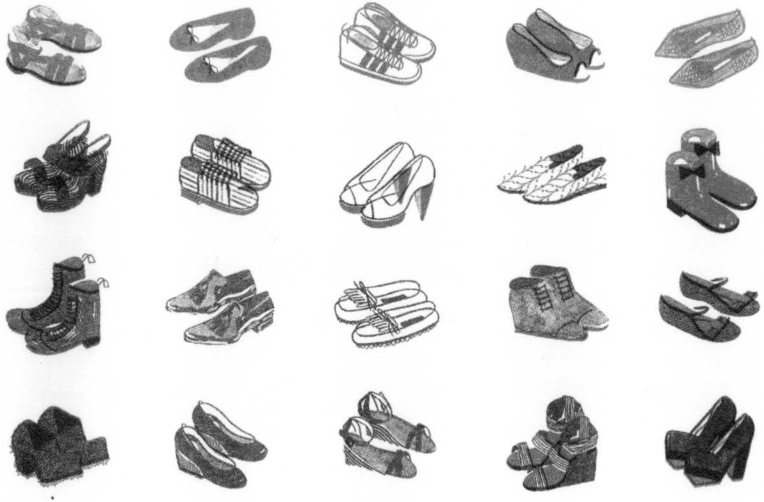

BY **HANNAH** K **LEE**

2

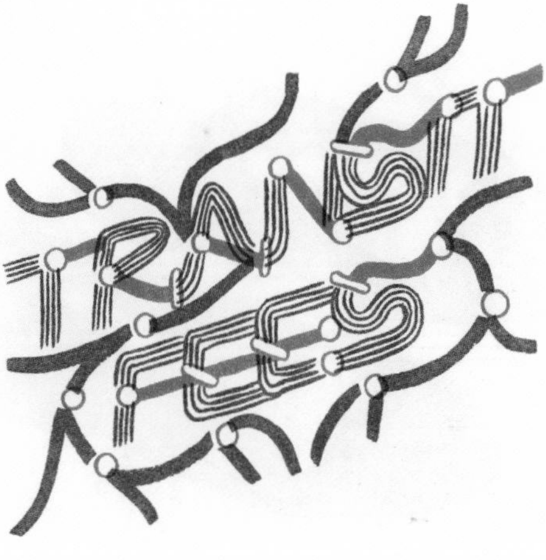
TRANSIT
FEES

CREDIT CARD
DEBT

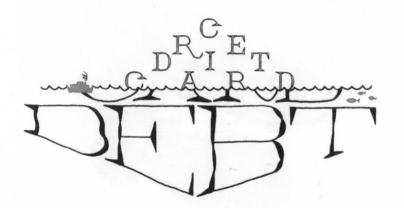

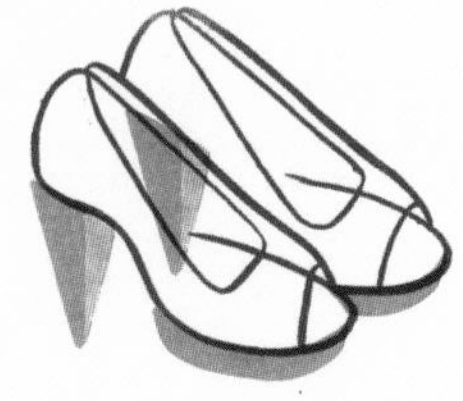

14

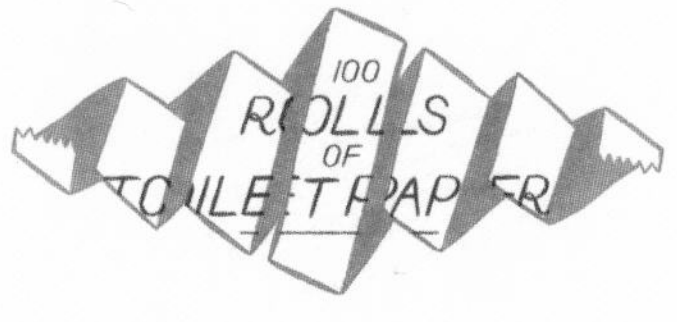
100
ROLLS
OF
TOILET PAPER

15

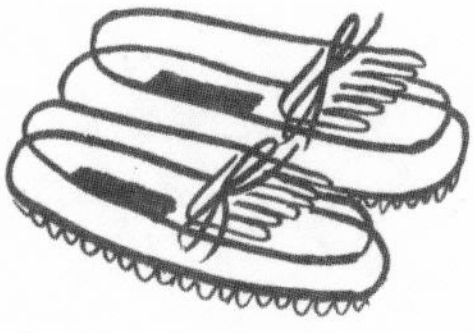

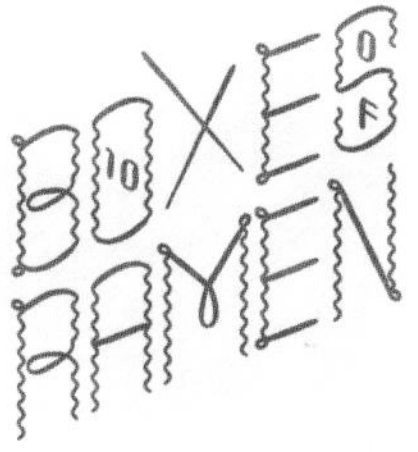
10
BOXES
OF
RAMEN

13

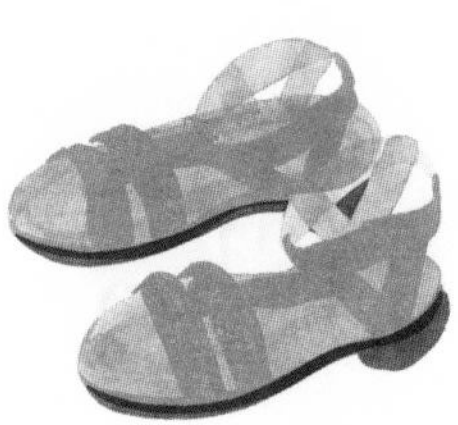

8

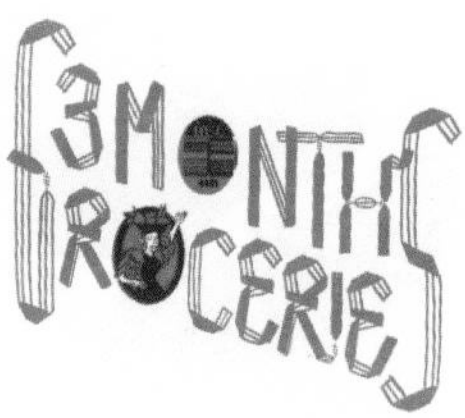
3 MONTHS
GROCERIES

9

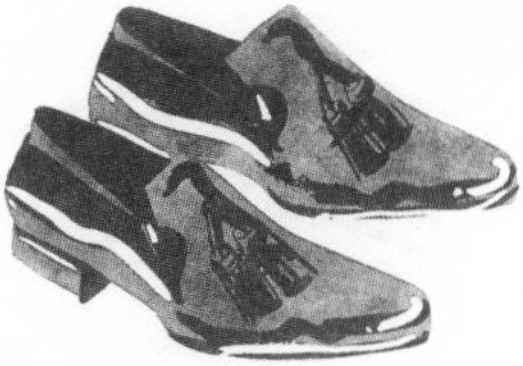

36

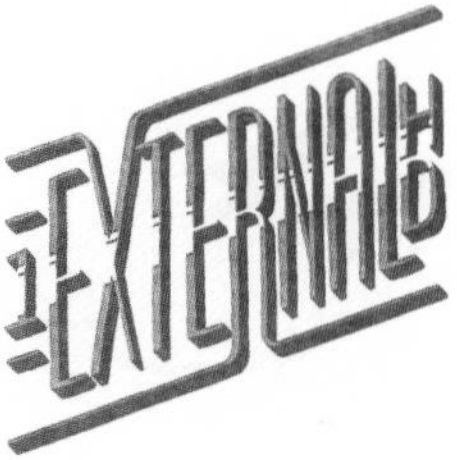
EXTERNAL

37

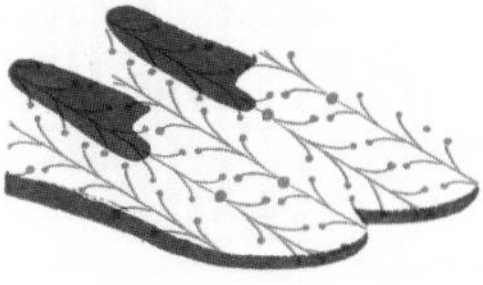

34

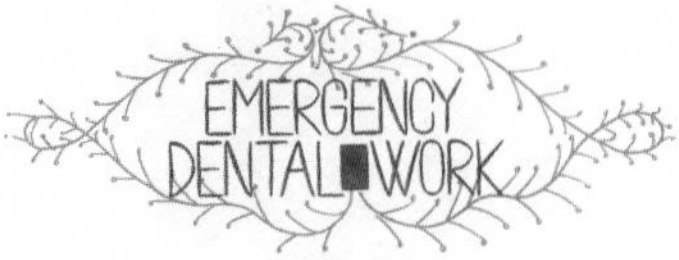
EMERGENCY
DENTAL WORK

35

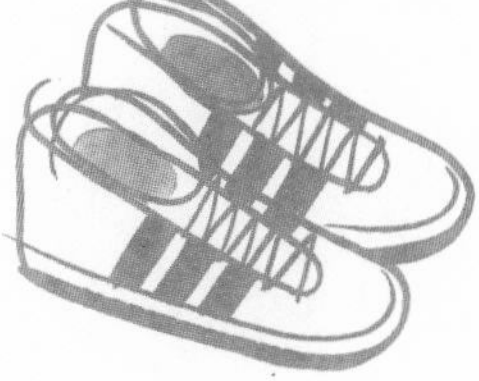

26

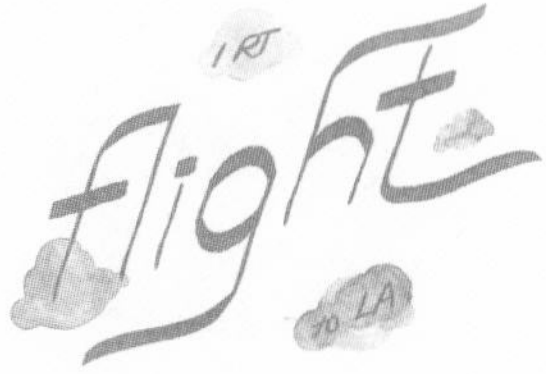
1 RT
flight
TO LA

27

20

STUDENT
LOANS

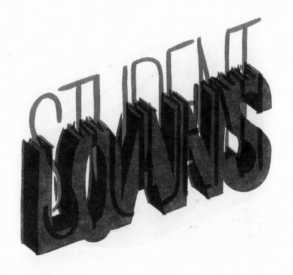

L 25 OADs LAUNDRY of

22

20
sandwiches

23

24

MAINTENANCE

25

32

UTILITIES

33

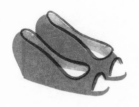

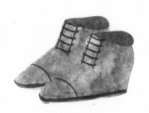

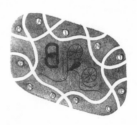

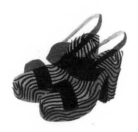

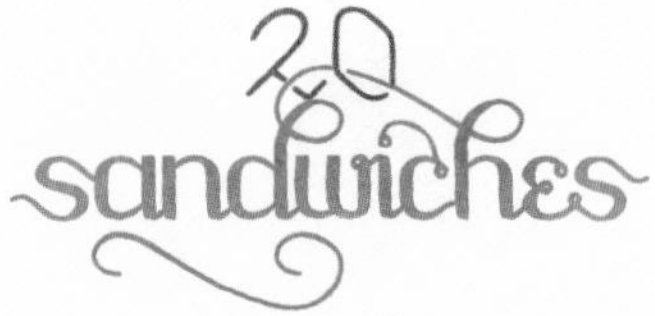

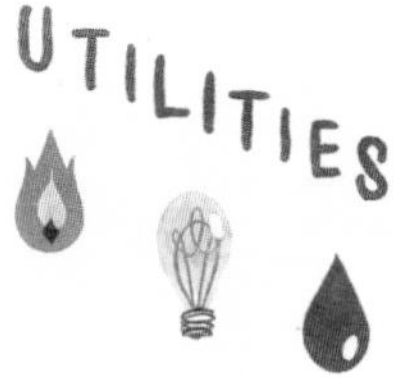

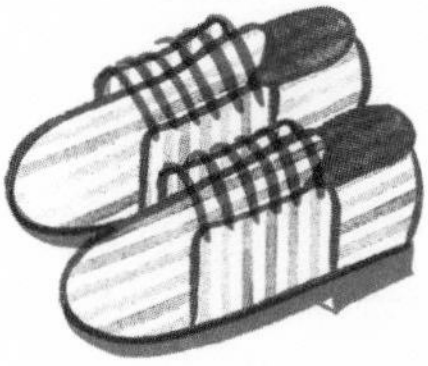

38

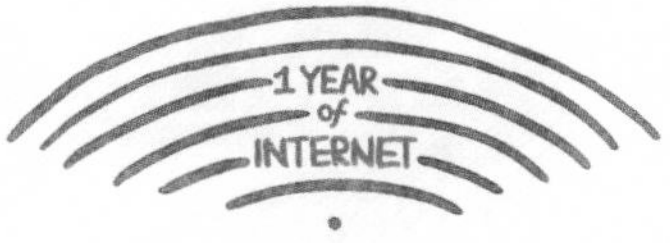
1 YEAR
of
INTERNET

39

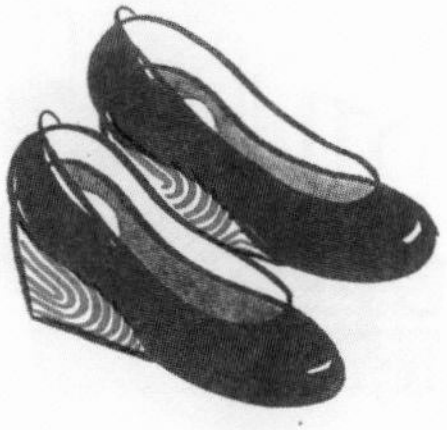

18

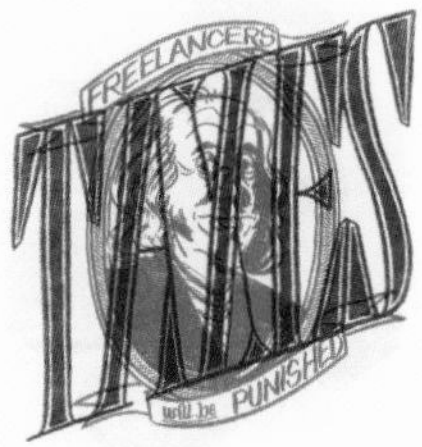
FREELANCERS
TAXES
will be PUNISHED

19

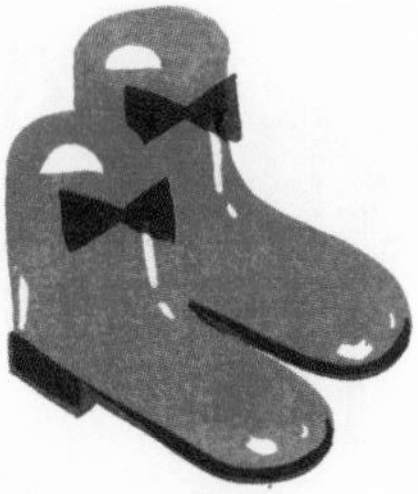

16

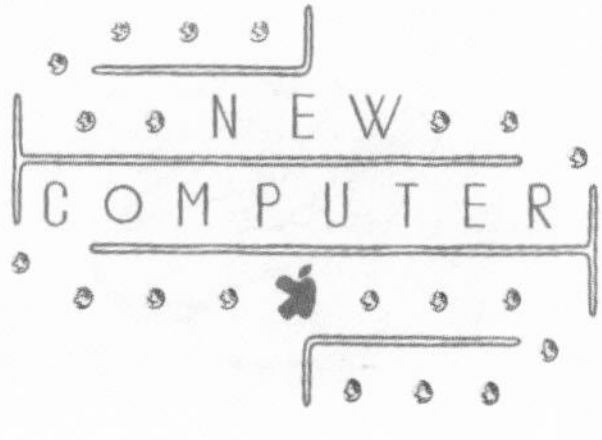
NEW
COMPUTER

17

1 dining experience

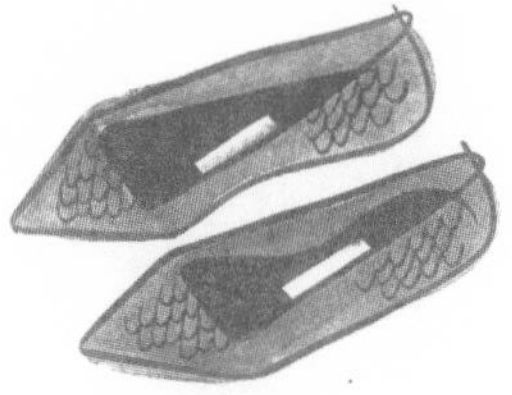

30

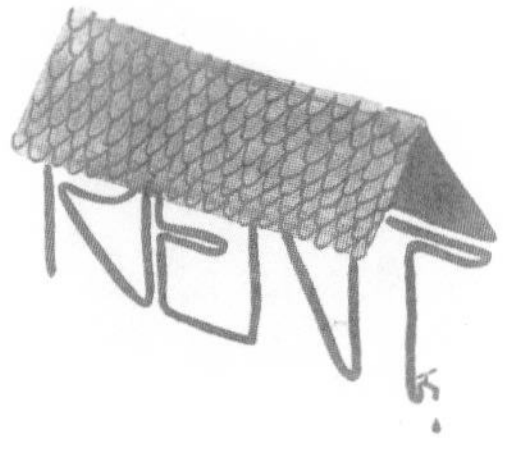
RENT

31

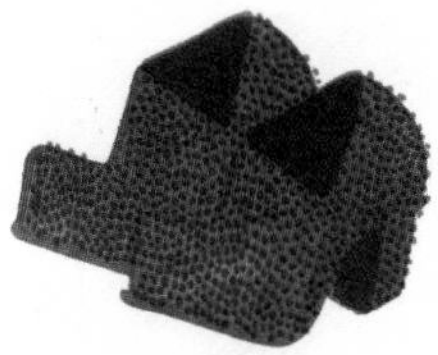

28

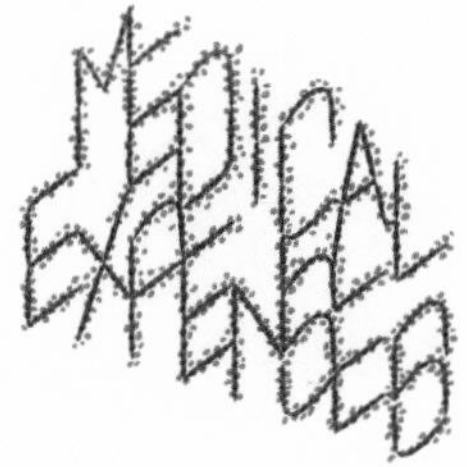
MEDICAL
EXPENSES

29

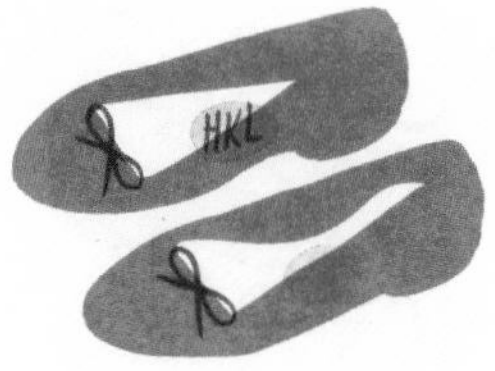
HKL

40

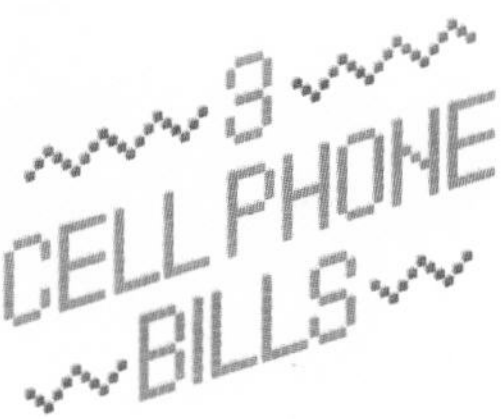
3
CELL PHONE
BILLS

41

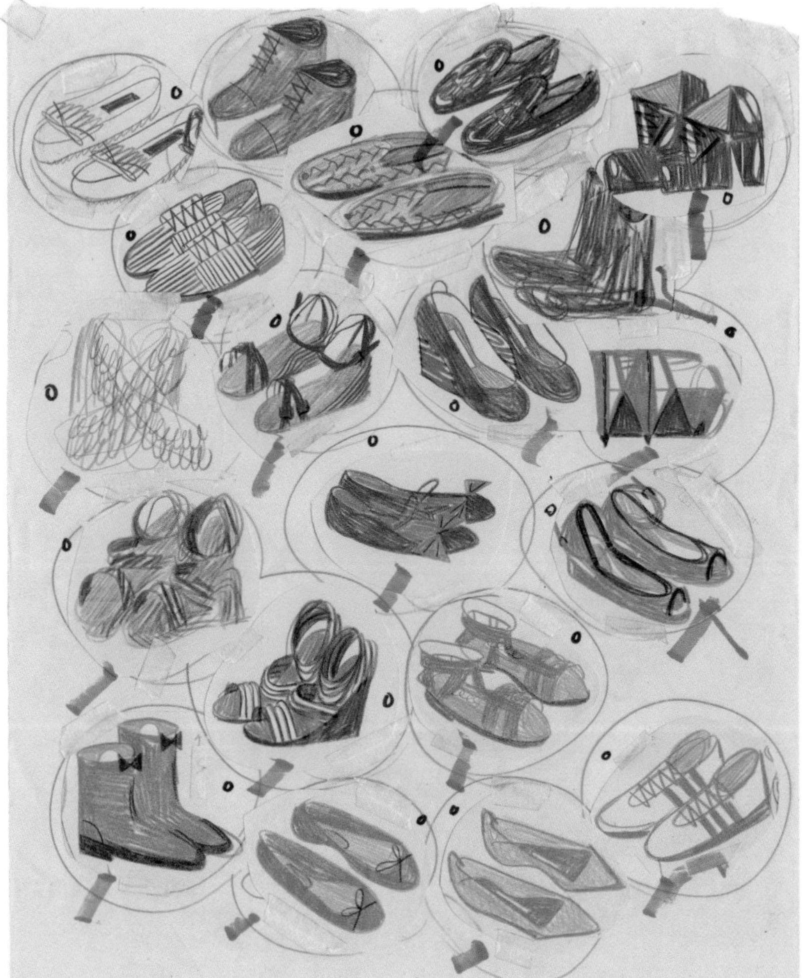

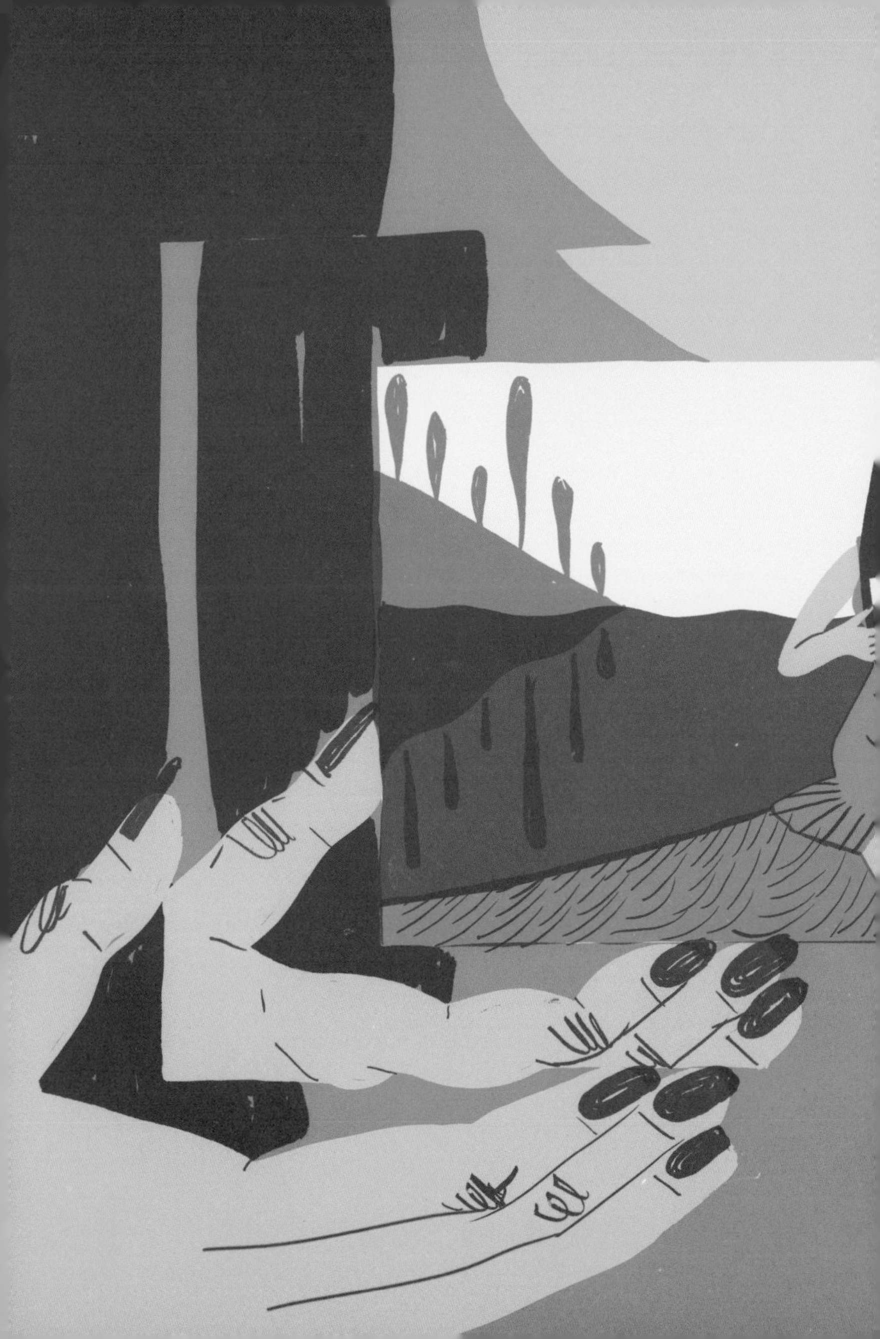

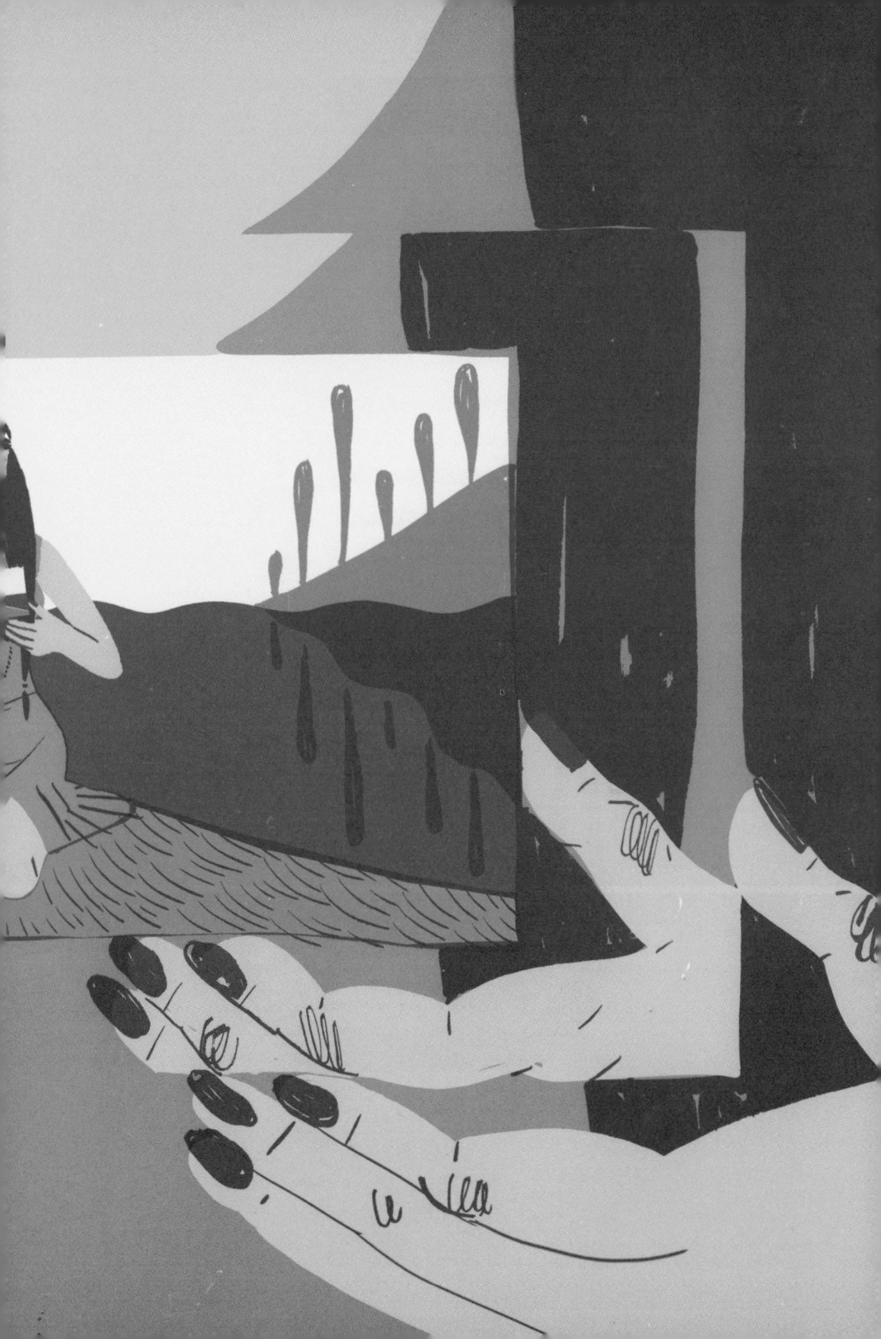

Issues #4

EVERYONE
ELSE
IS

YOUNGER

AND
MORE
TALENTED

by Hannah K. Lee

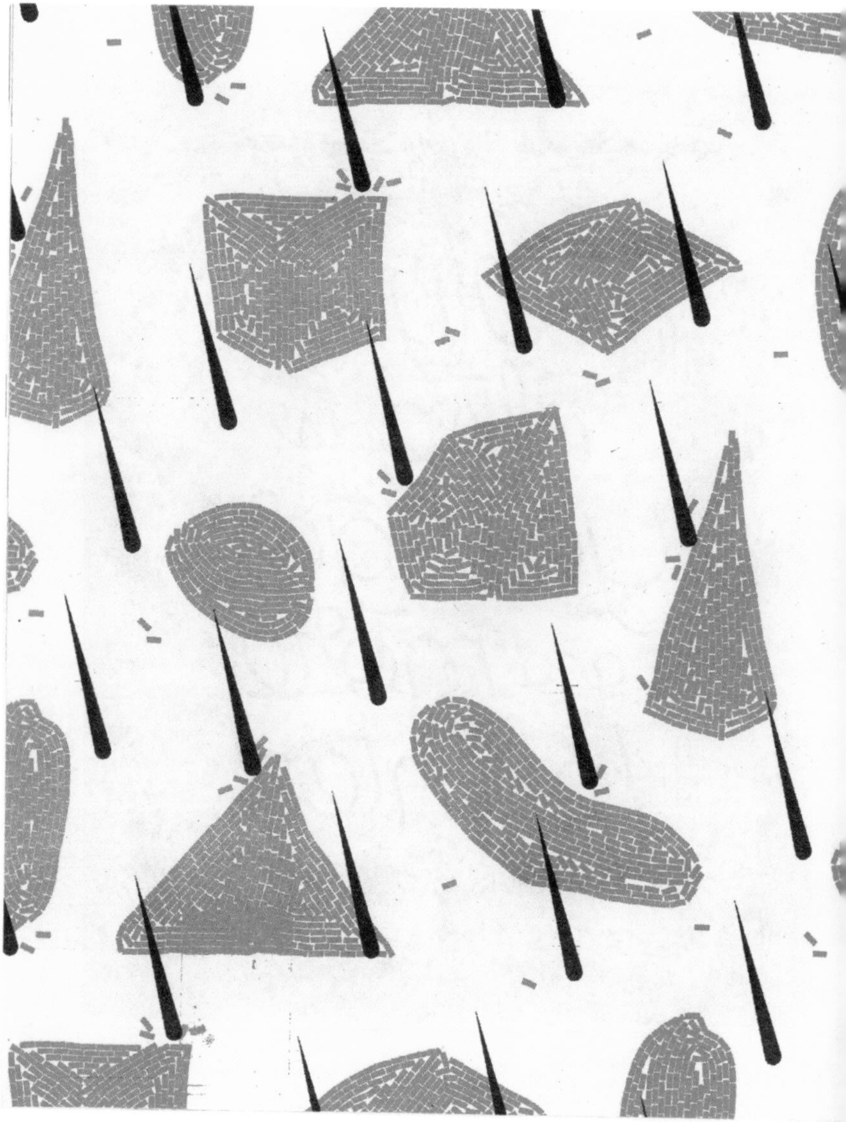

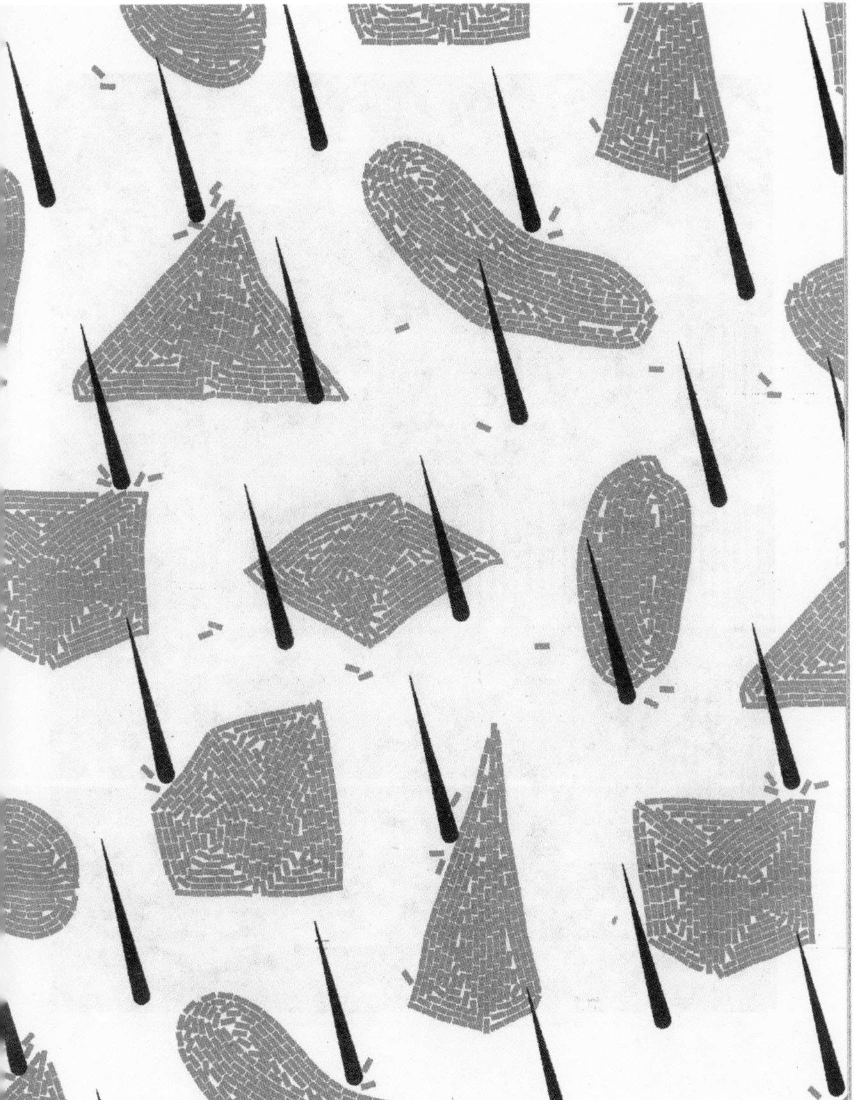

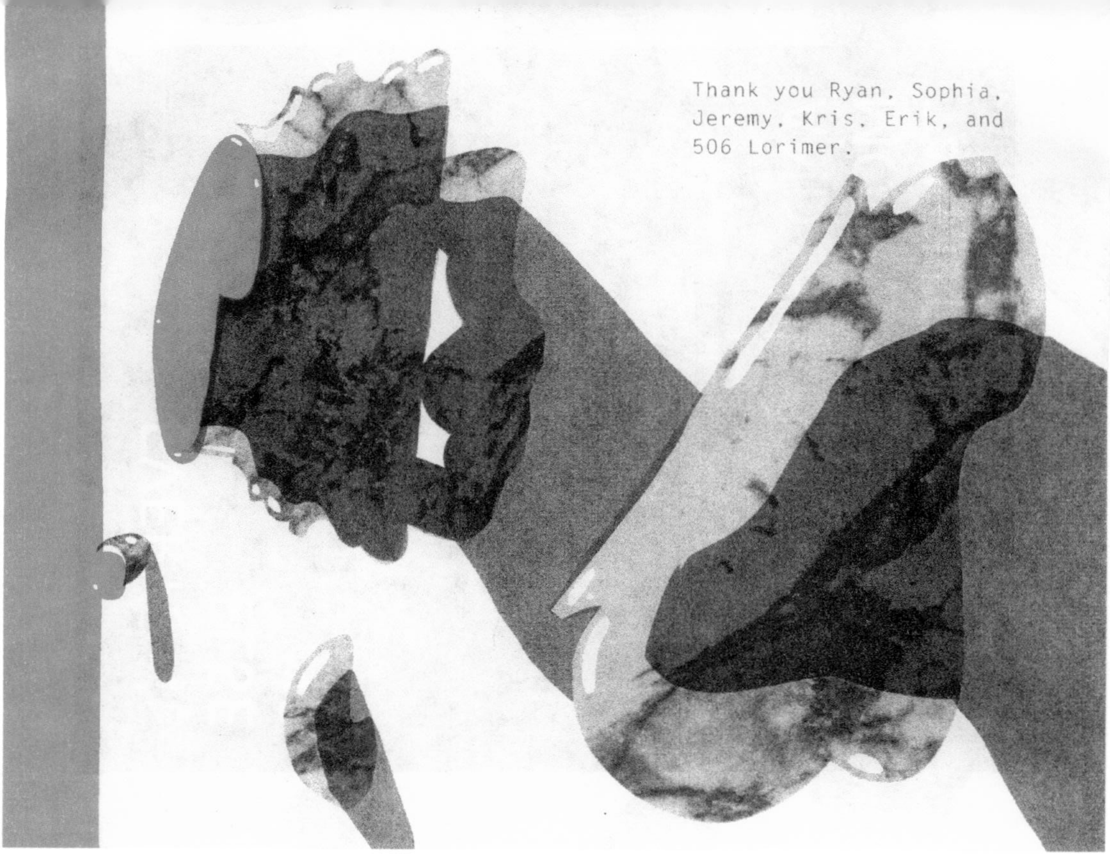

Thank you Ryan, Sophia, Jeremy, Kris, Erik, and 506 Lorimer.

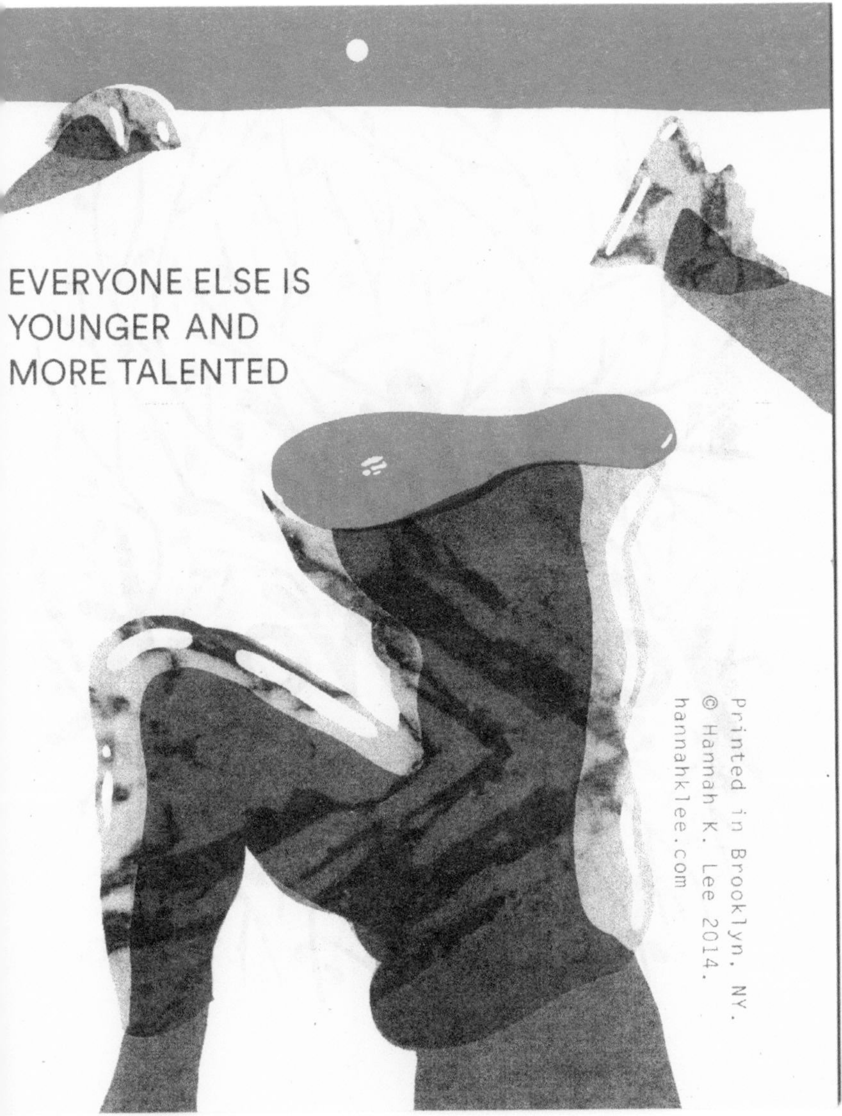
EVERYONE ELSE IS
YOUNGER AND
MORE TALENTED

Printed in Brooklyn, NY.

hannahklee.com

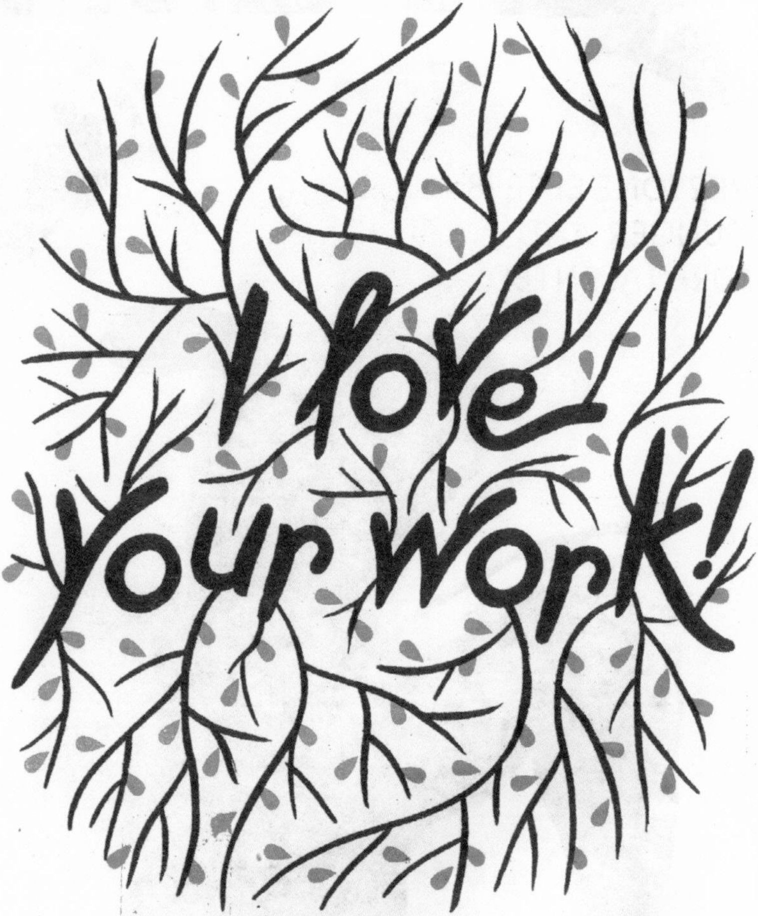
I love
your work!

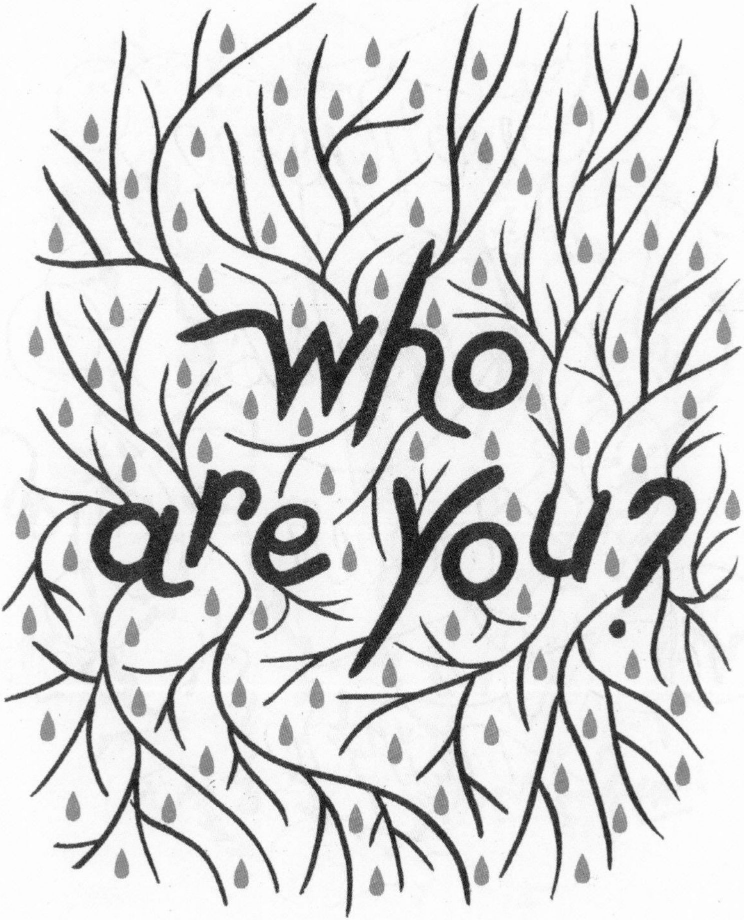
who
are you?

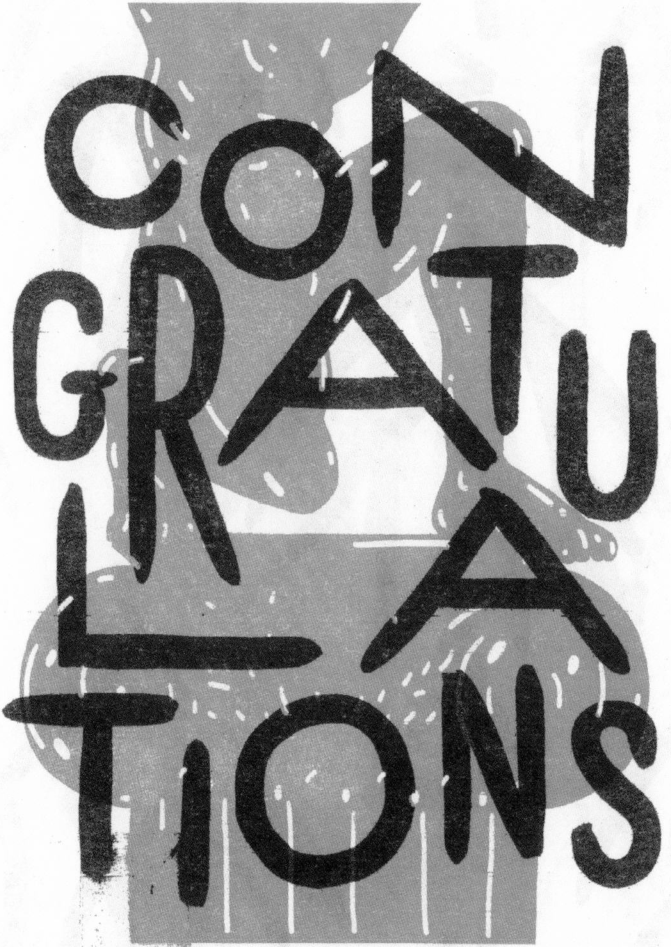
CON
GRATU
LA
TIONS

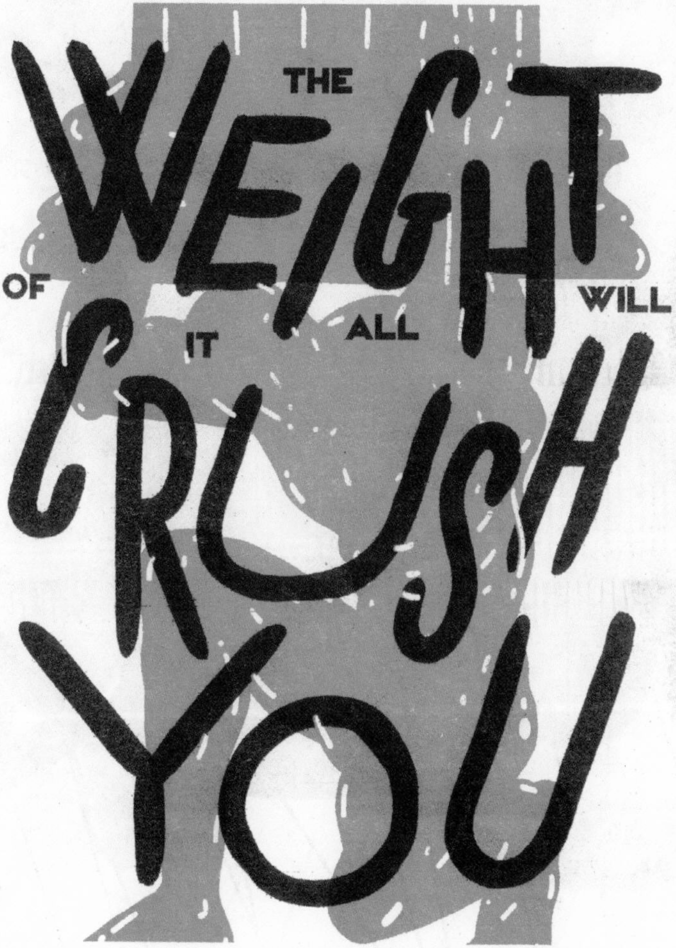
THE
WEIGHT
OF
IT
ALL
WILL
CRUSH
YOU

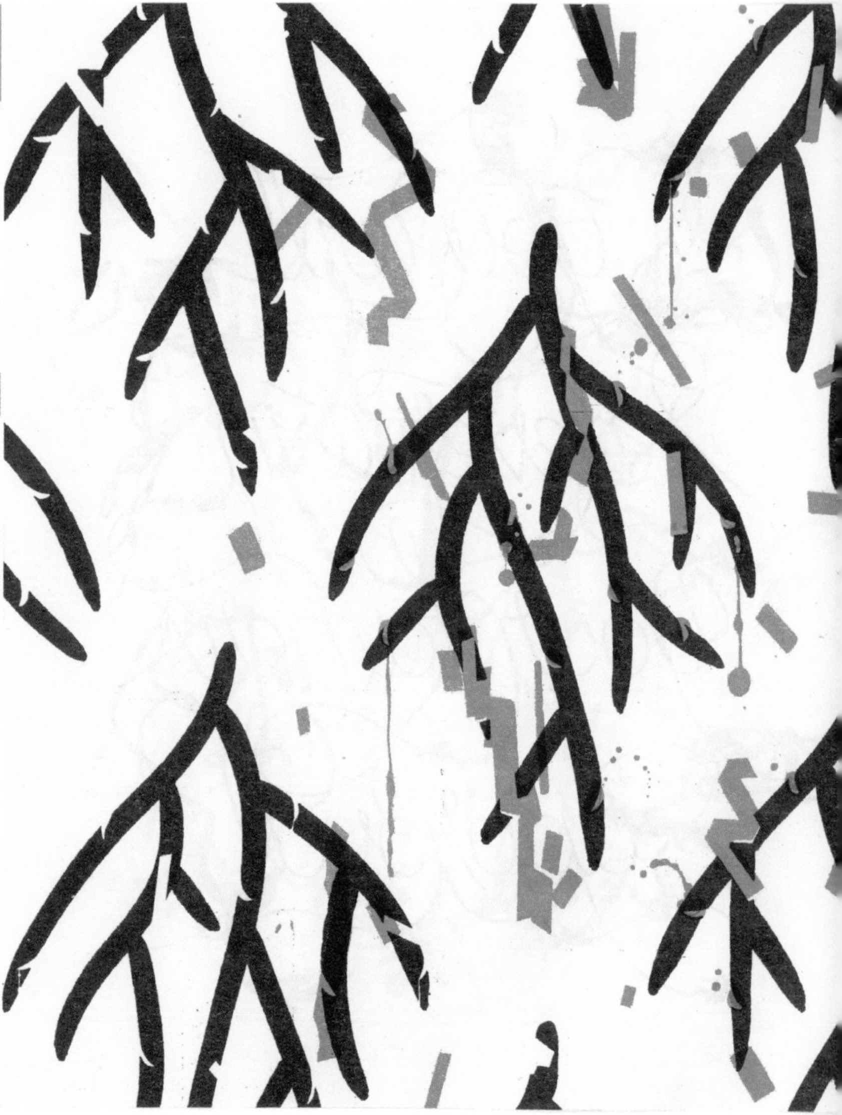

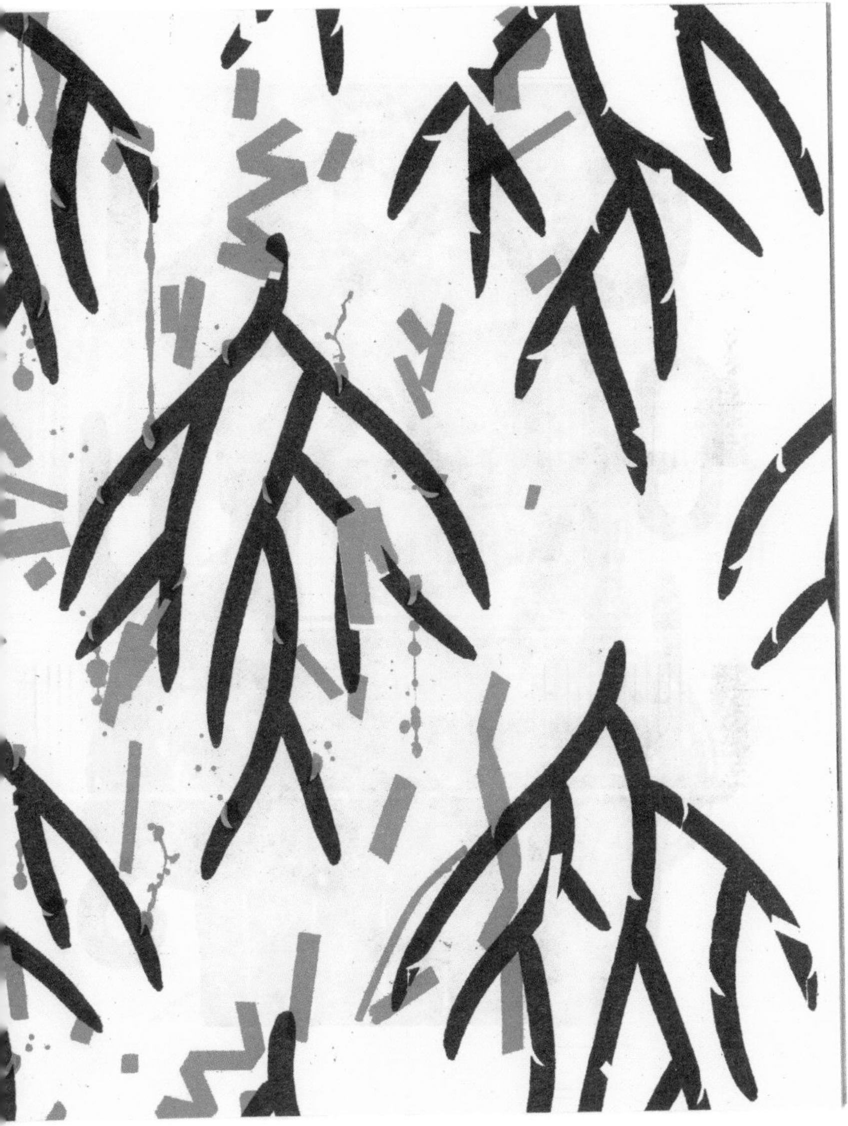

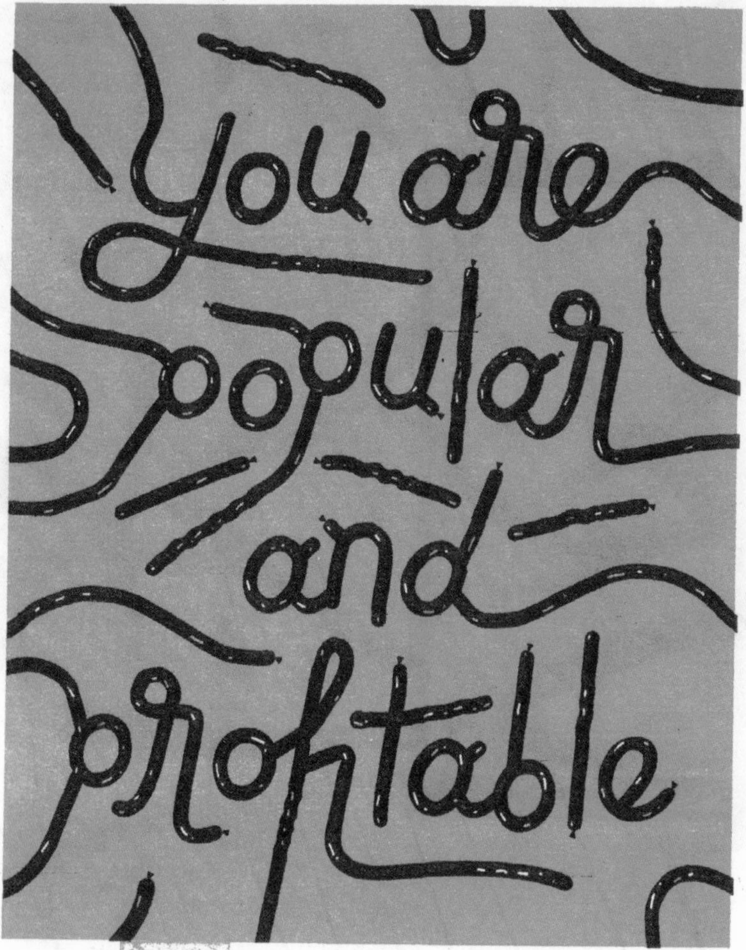
You are
popular
and
profitable

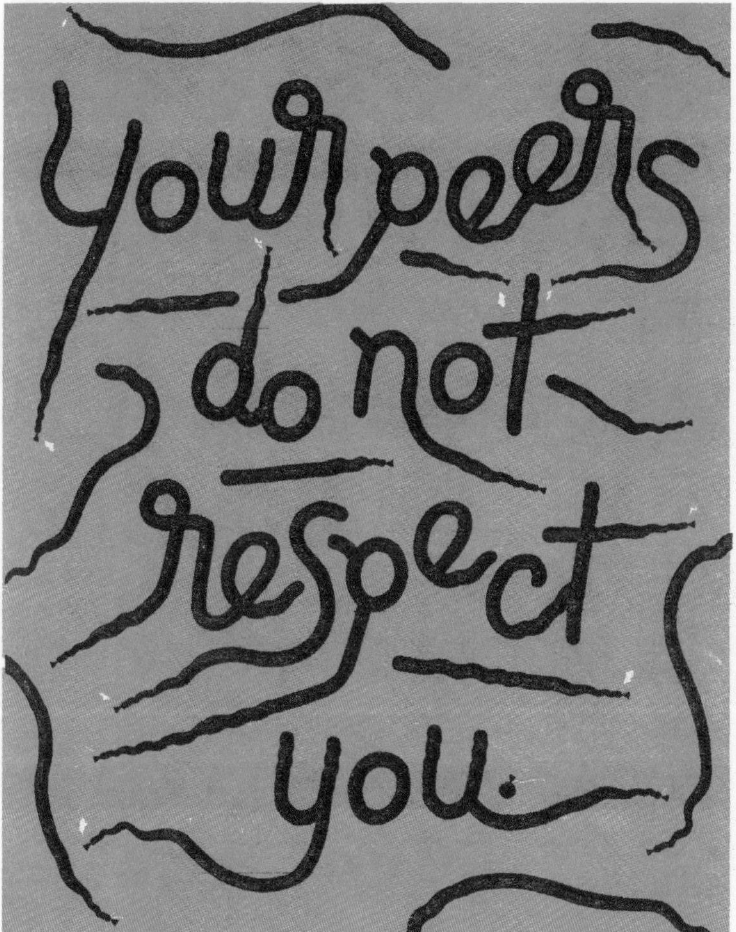
your peers
do not
respect
you.

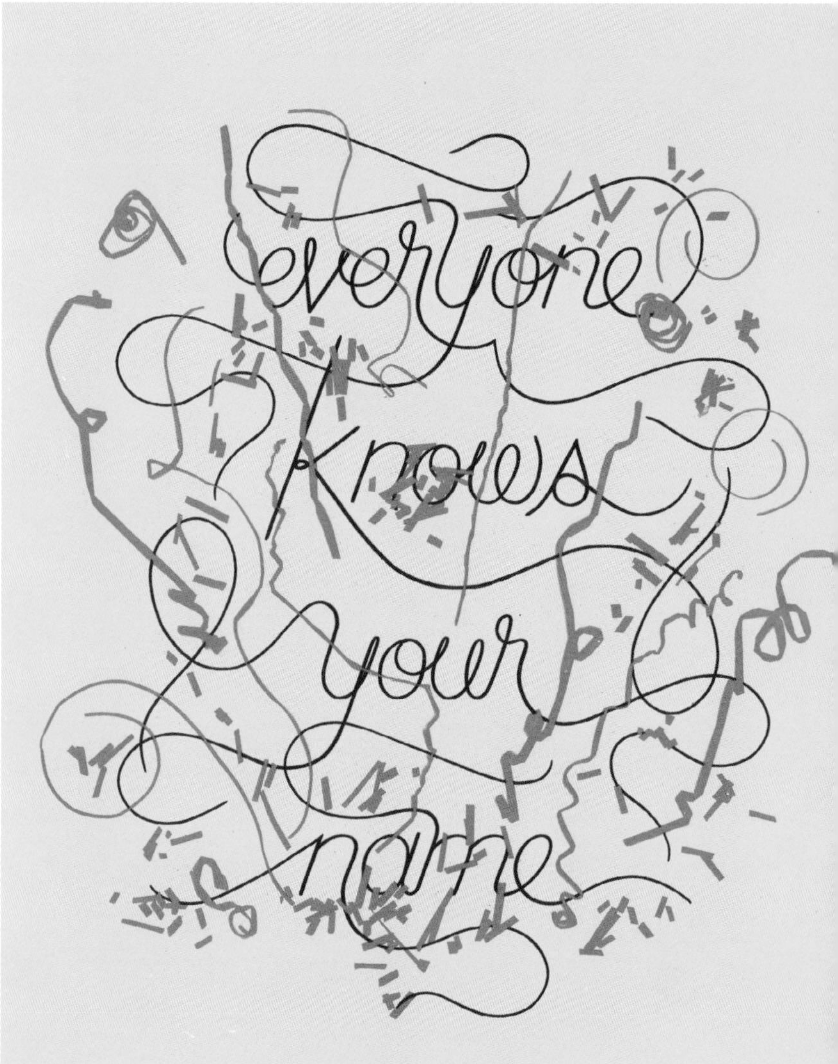
everyone
knows
your
name

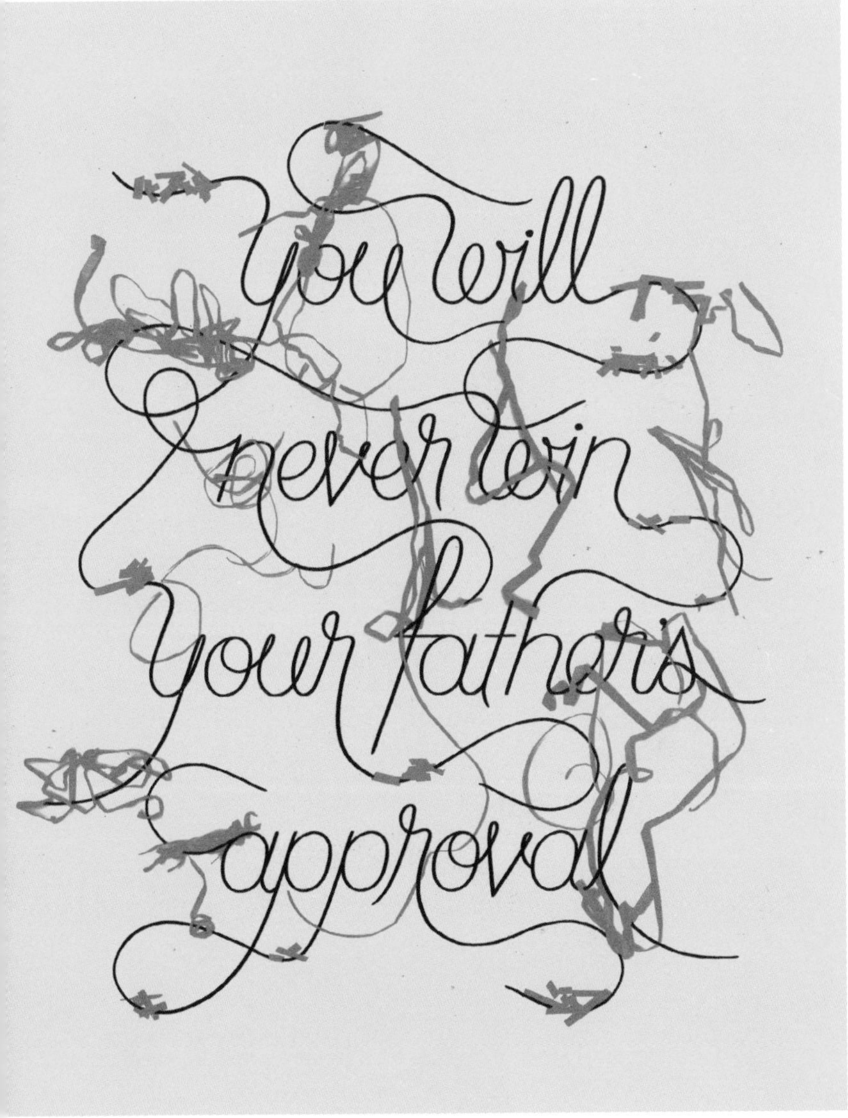
you will
never win
your father's
approval

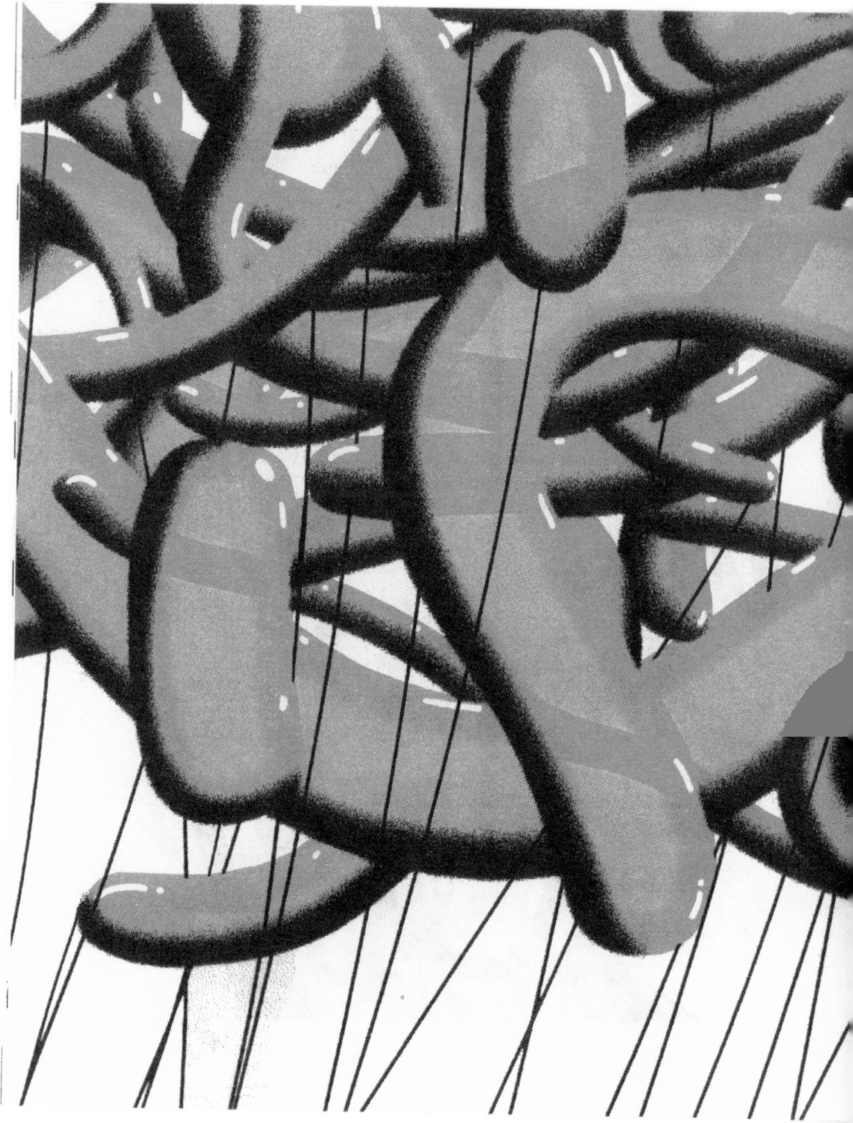

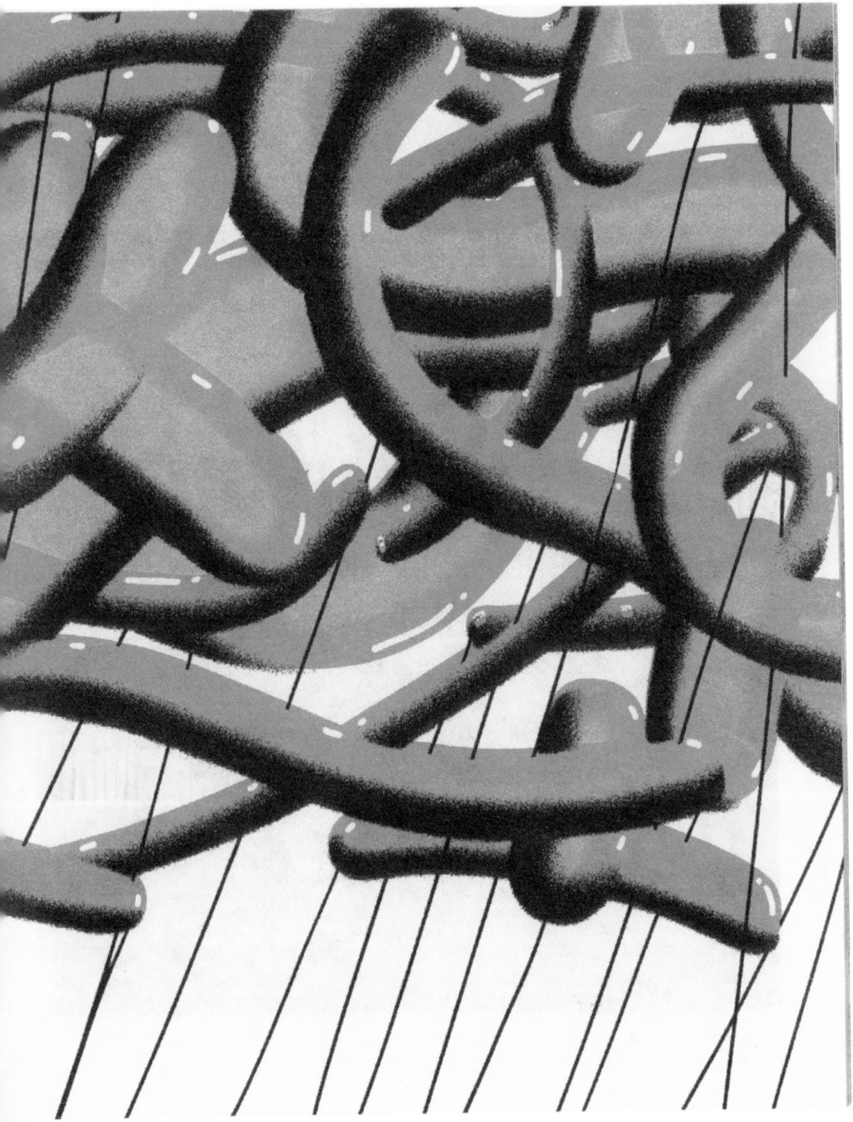

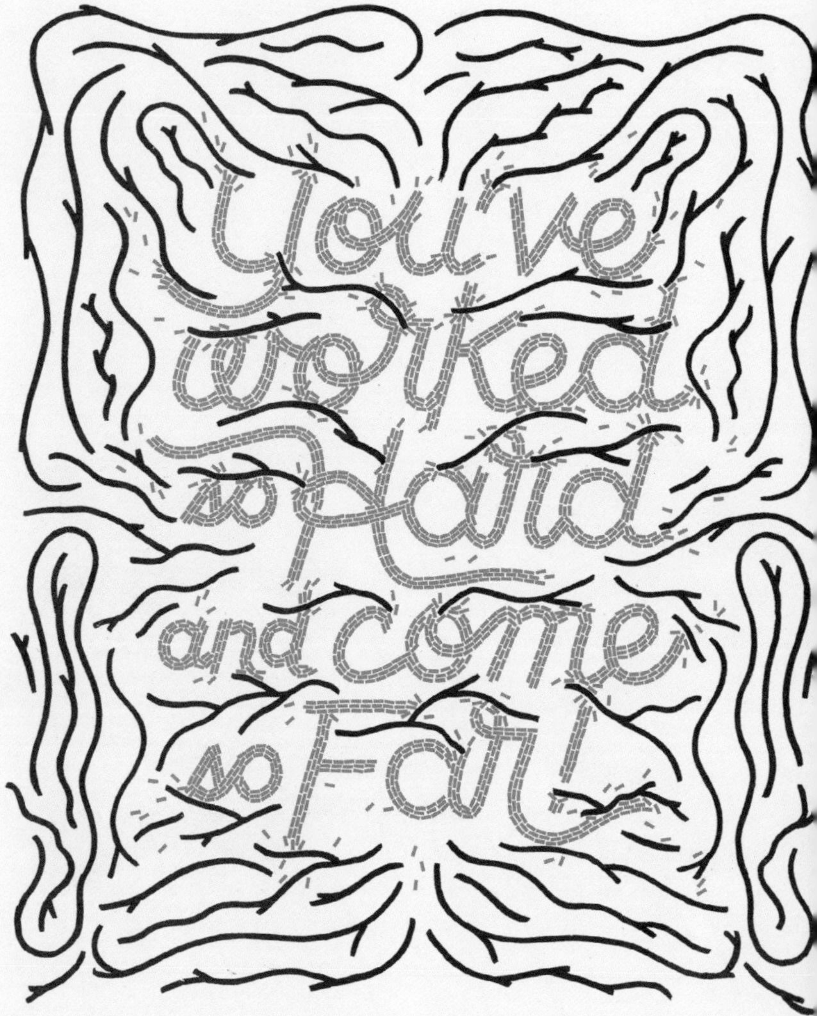
You've worked so Hard and come so Far!

Everyone else is younger and more Talented.

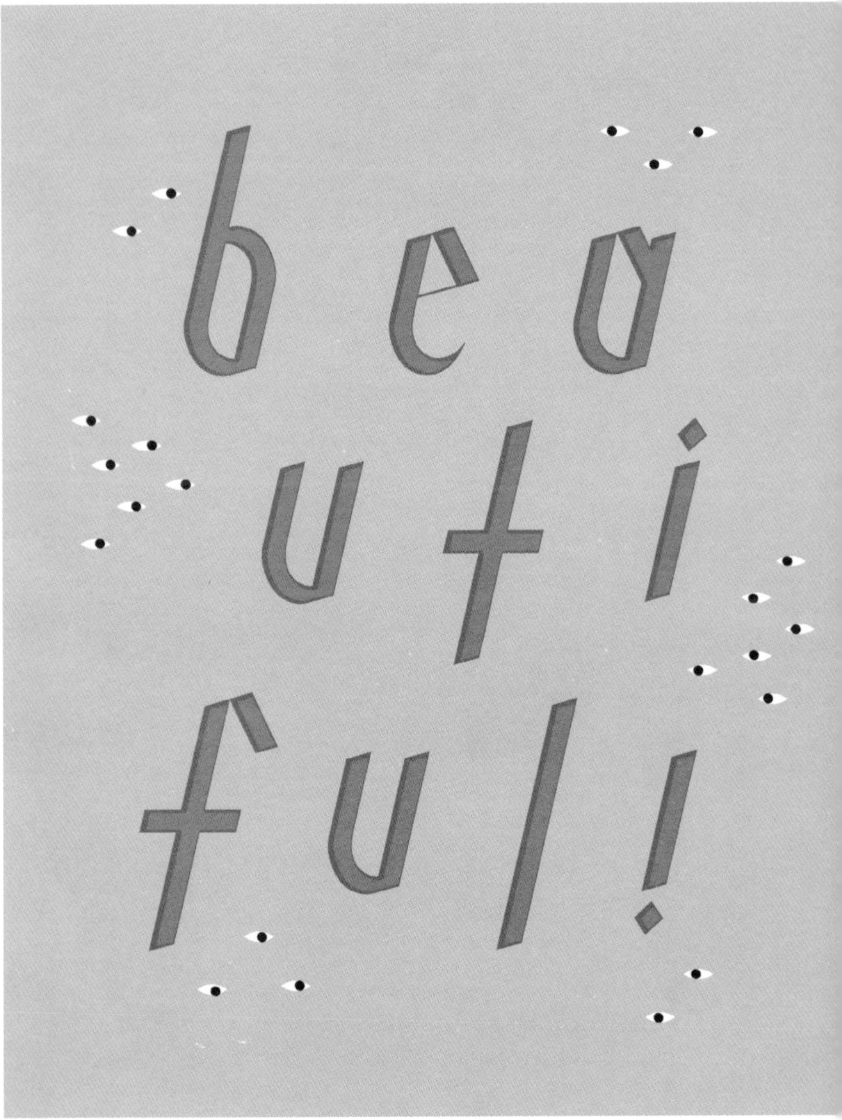
bea
uti
ful!

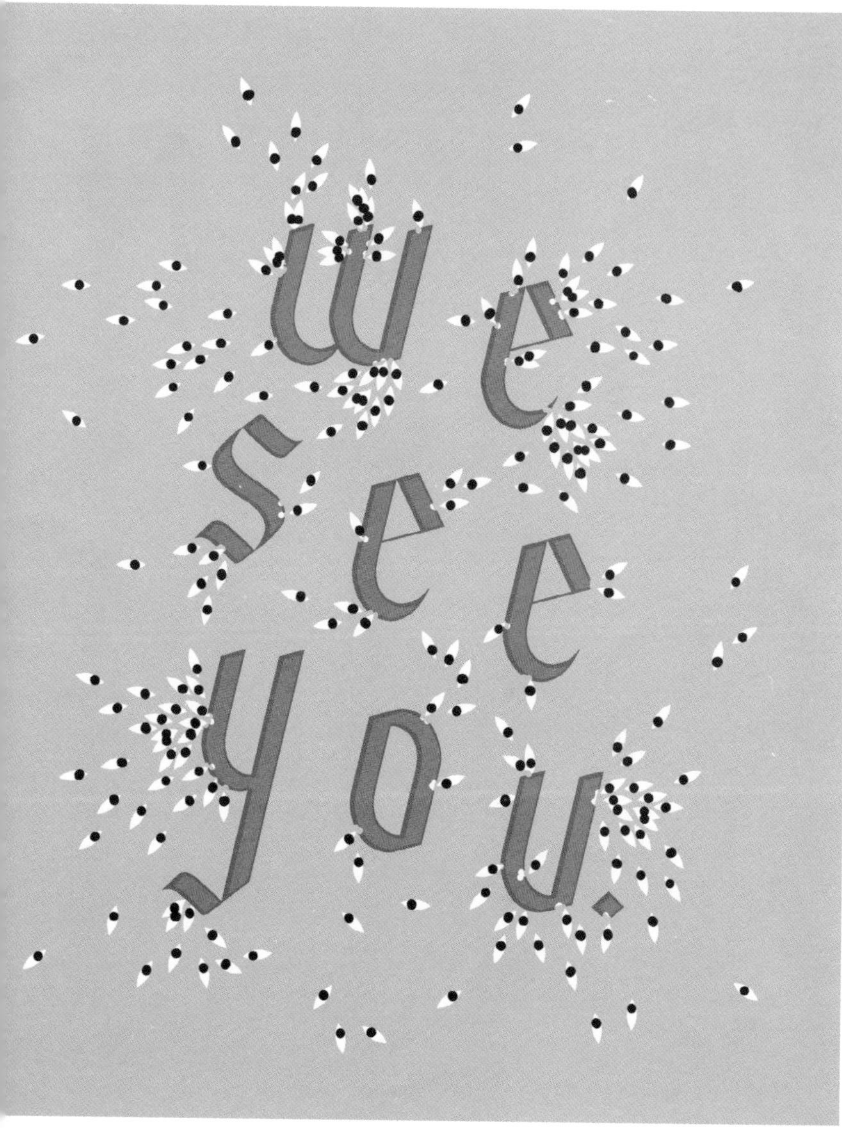
We
see
you.

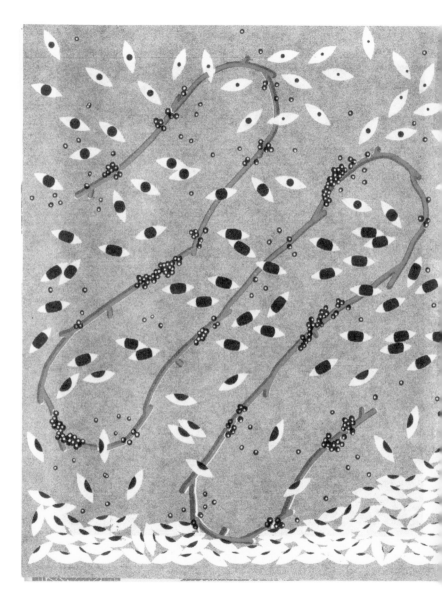

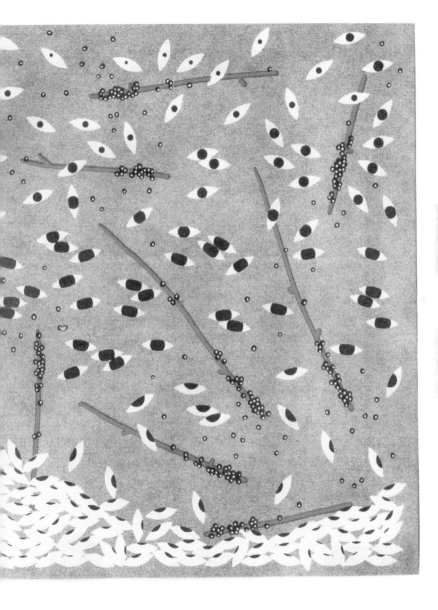

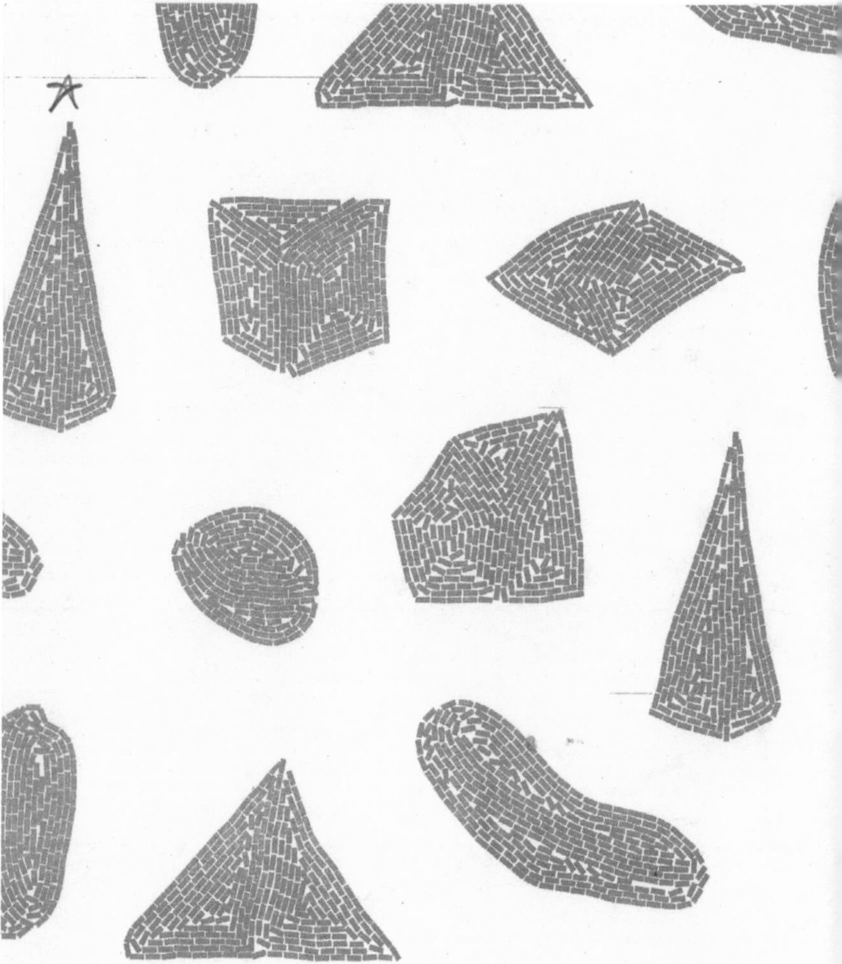

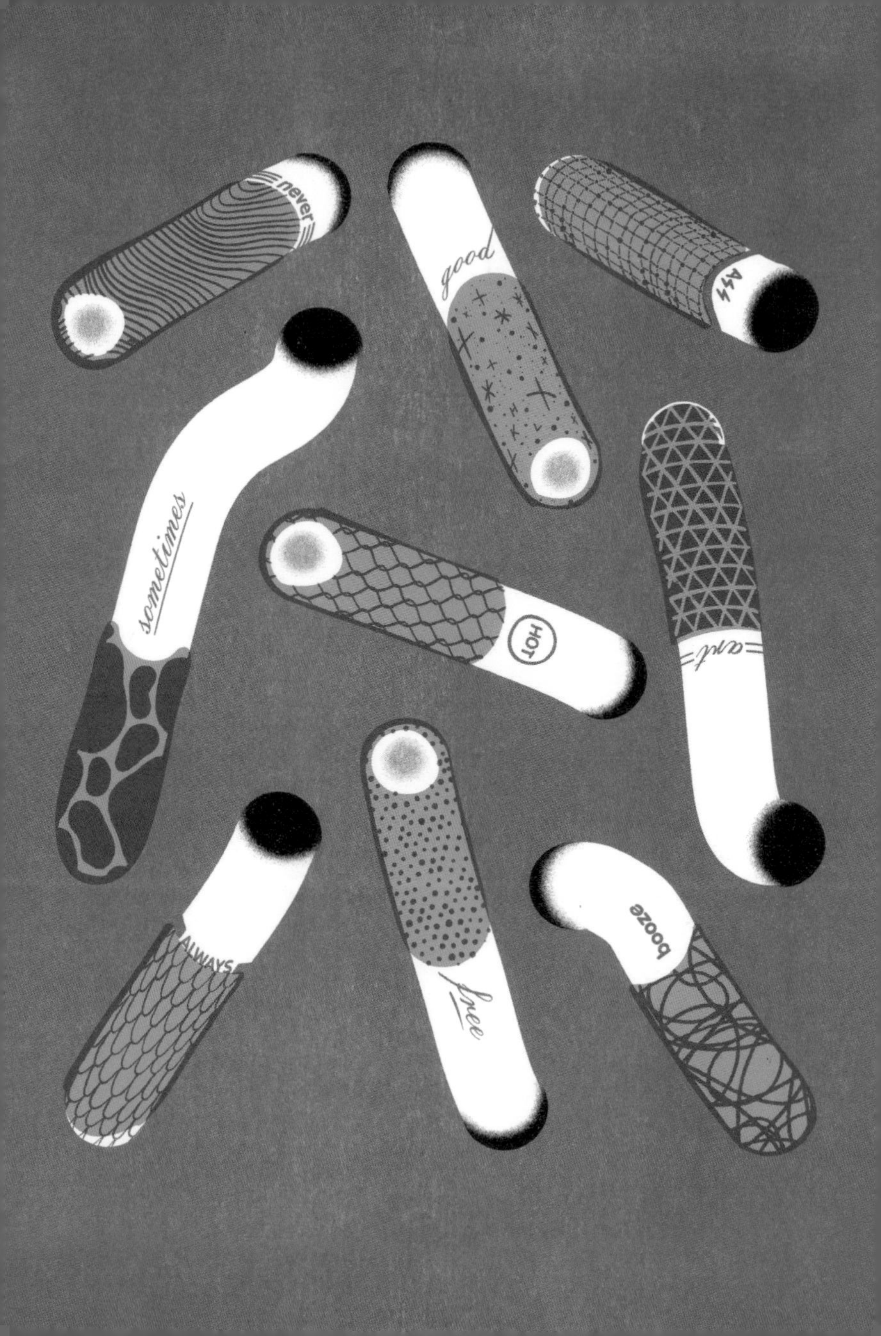
never
good
A44
sometimes
HOT
and
ALWAYS
free
booze

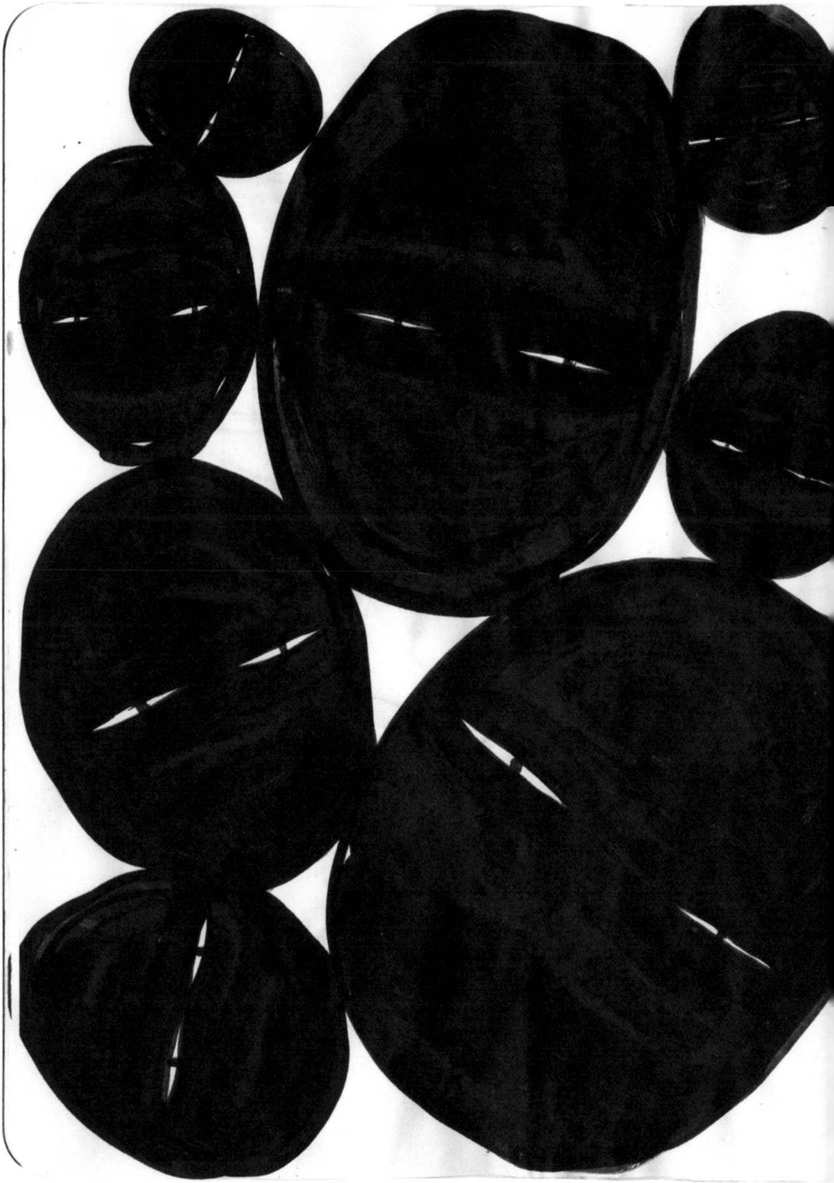

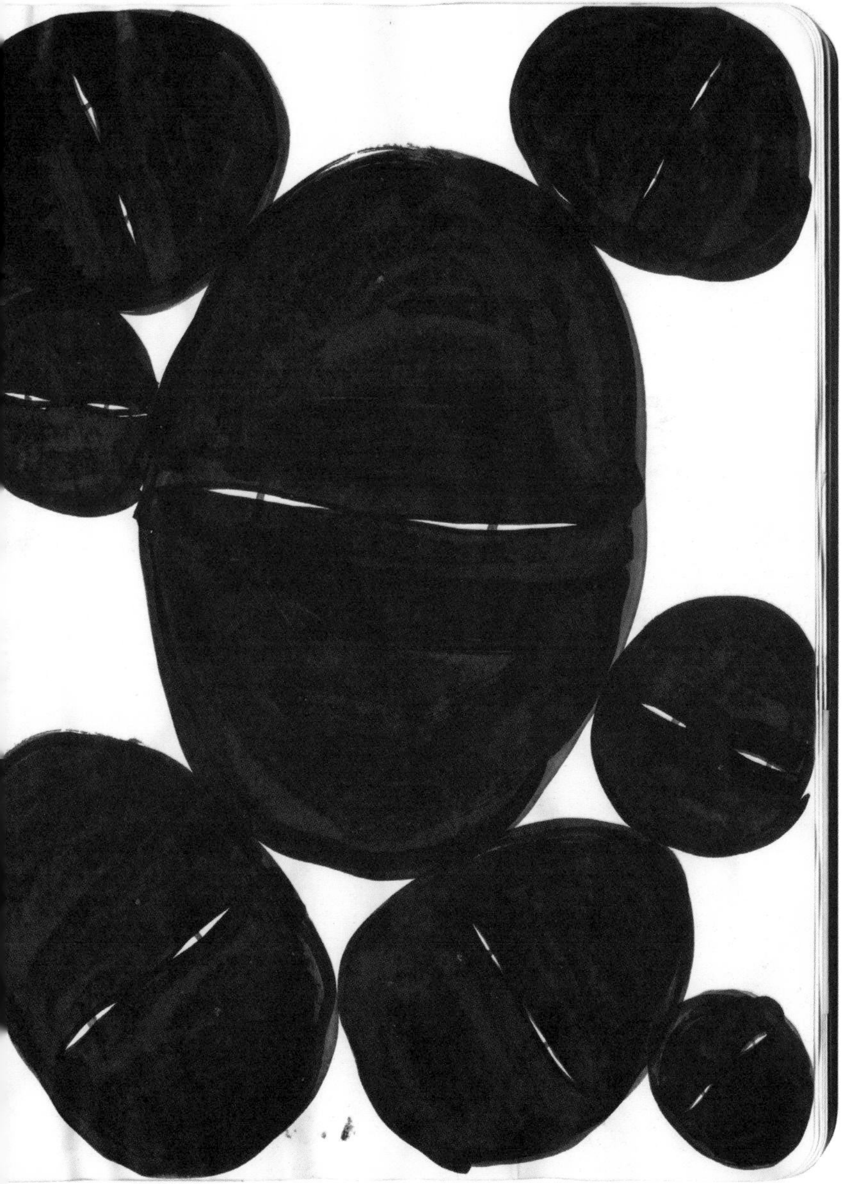

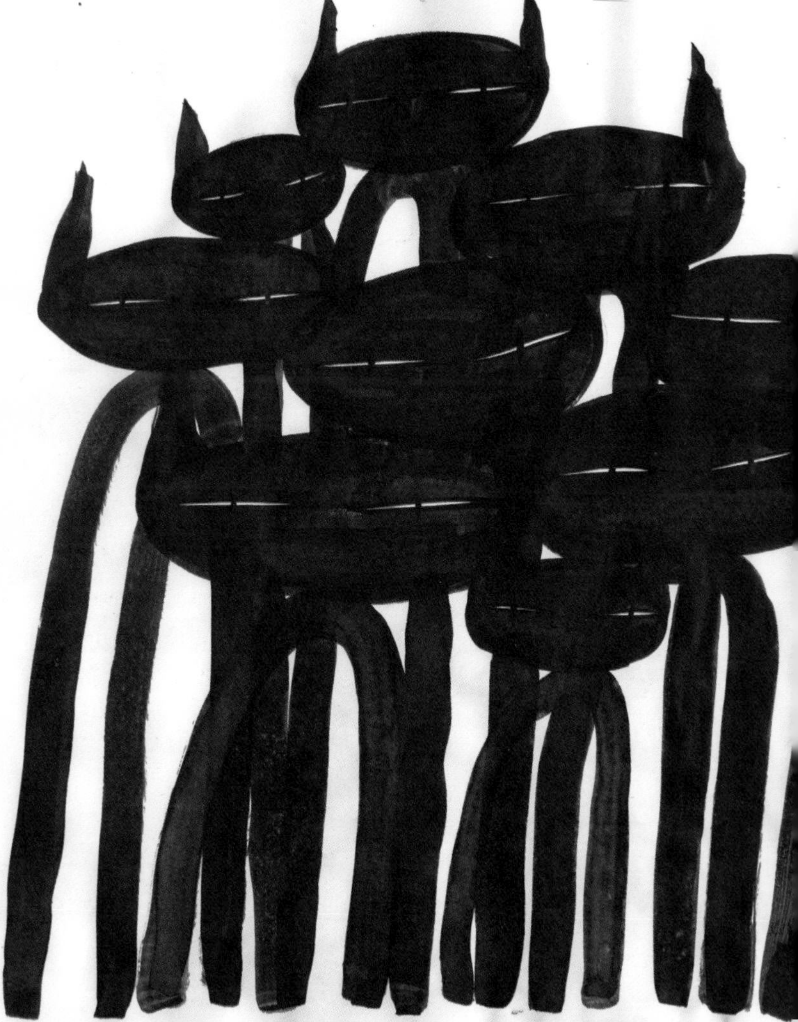

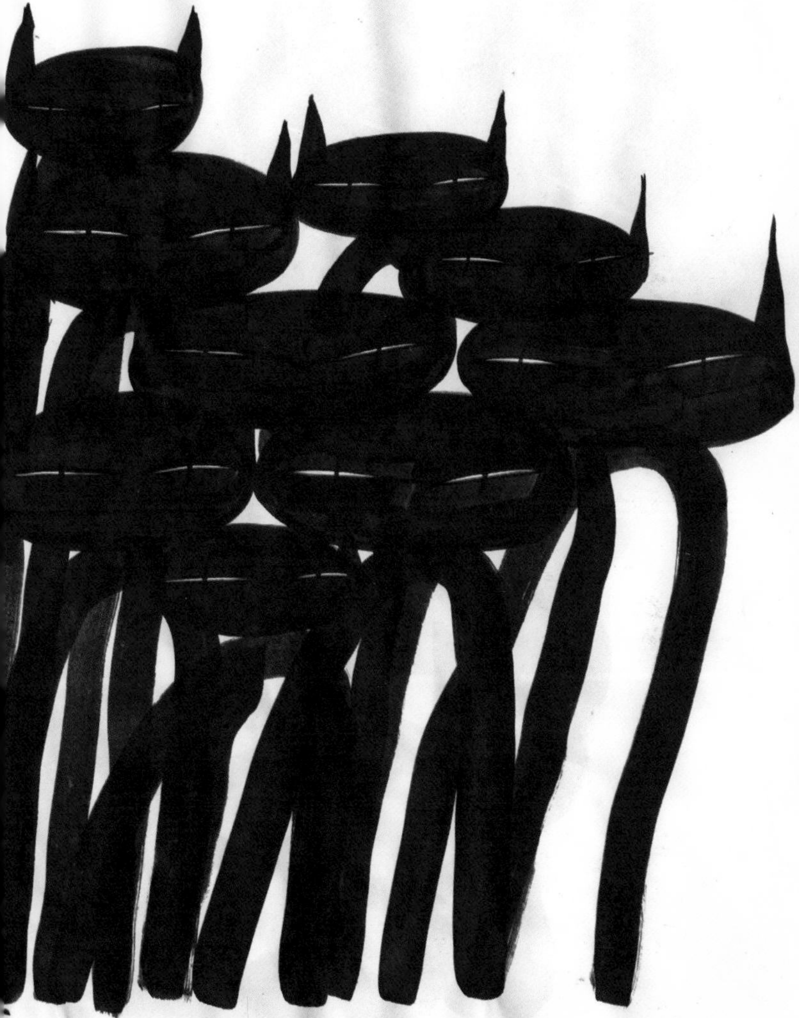

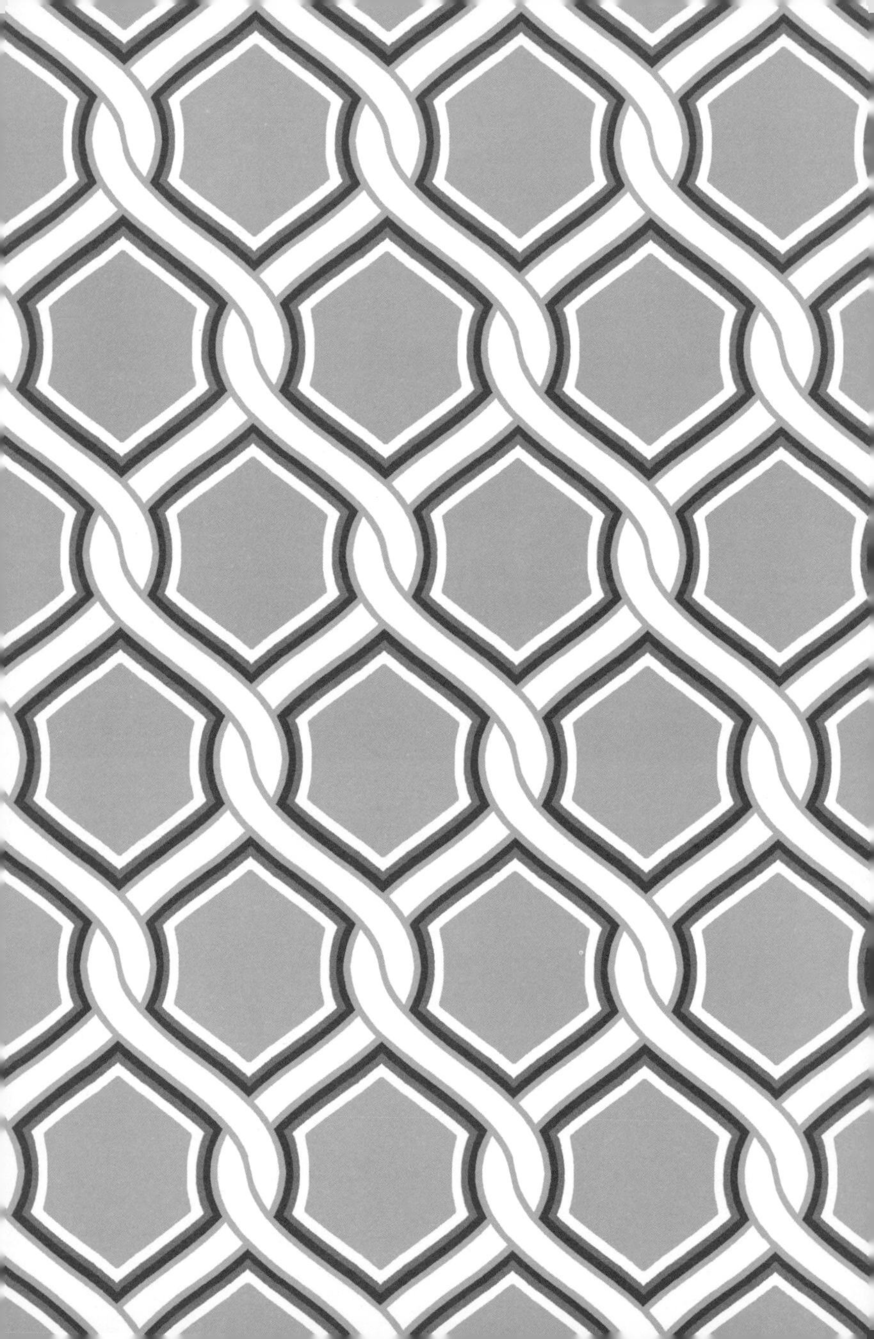

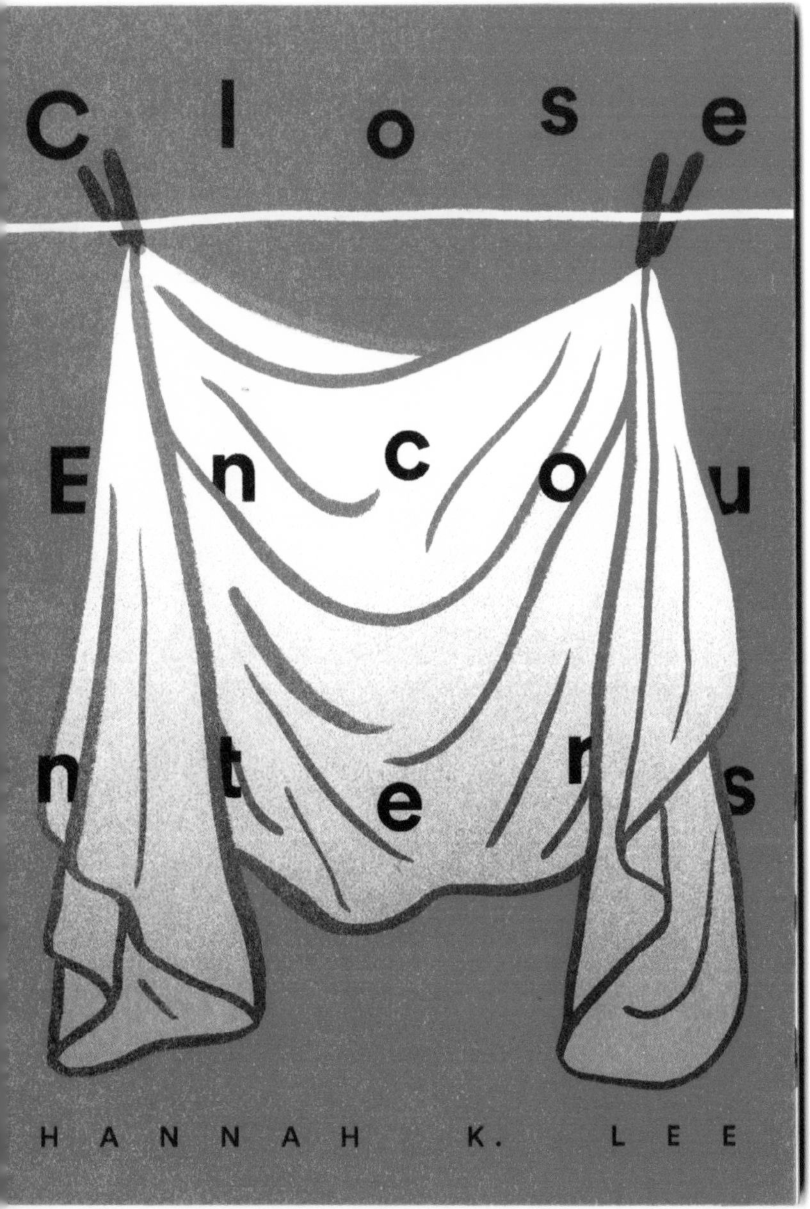
Close
Encounters
HANNAH K. LEE

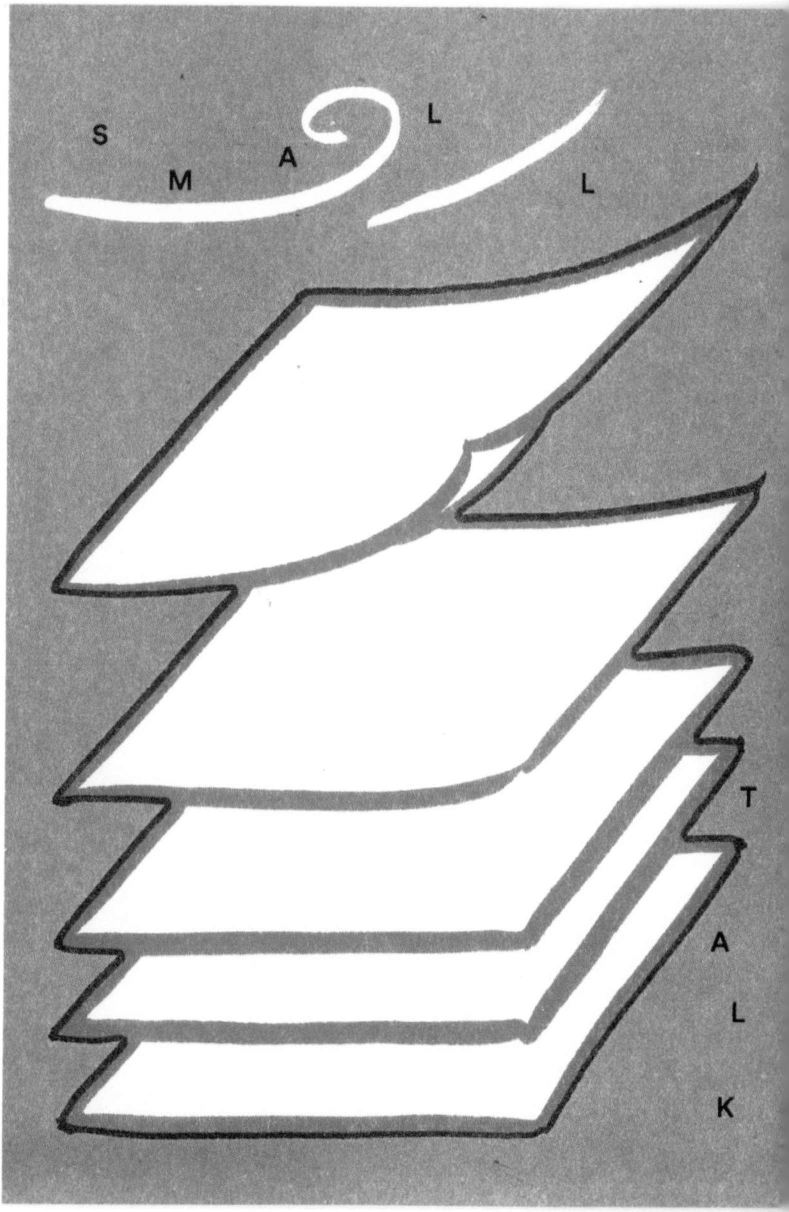
SMALL
TALK

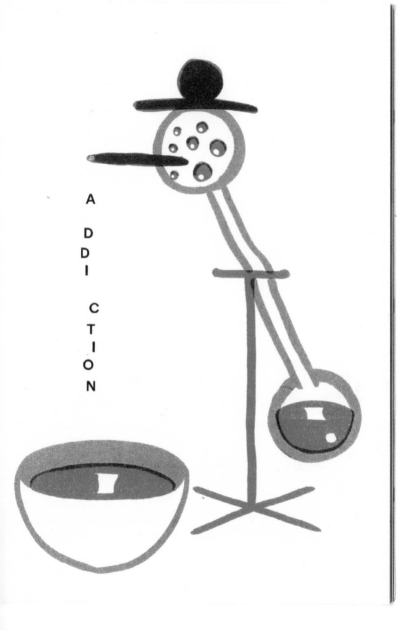

A
D
D
I
C
T
I
O
N

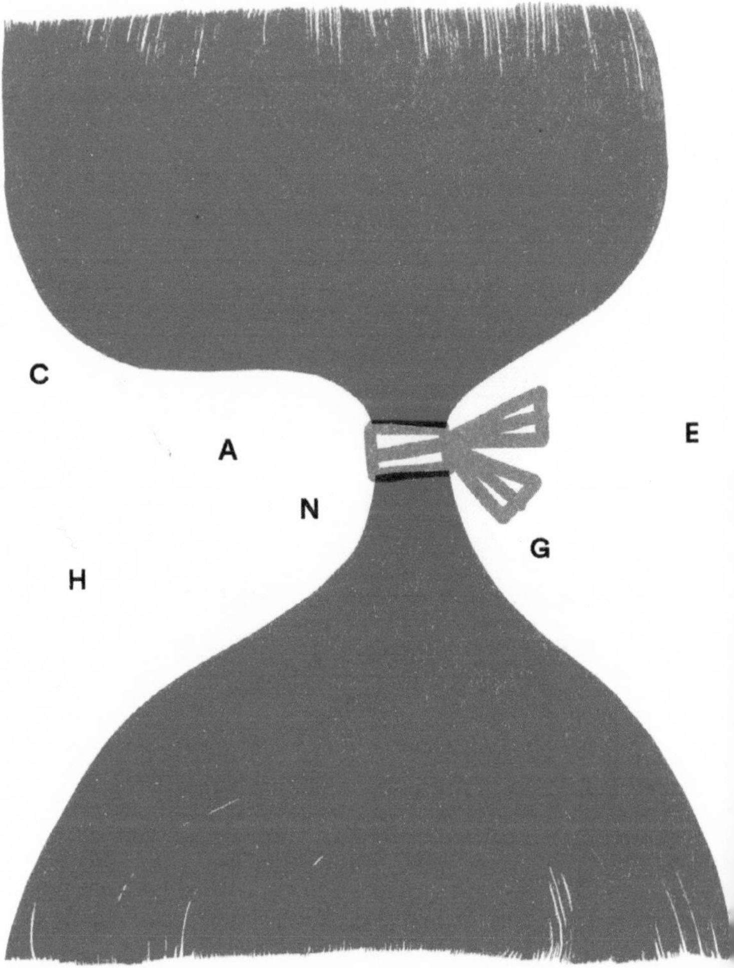
C
A
E
N
G
H

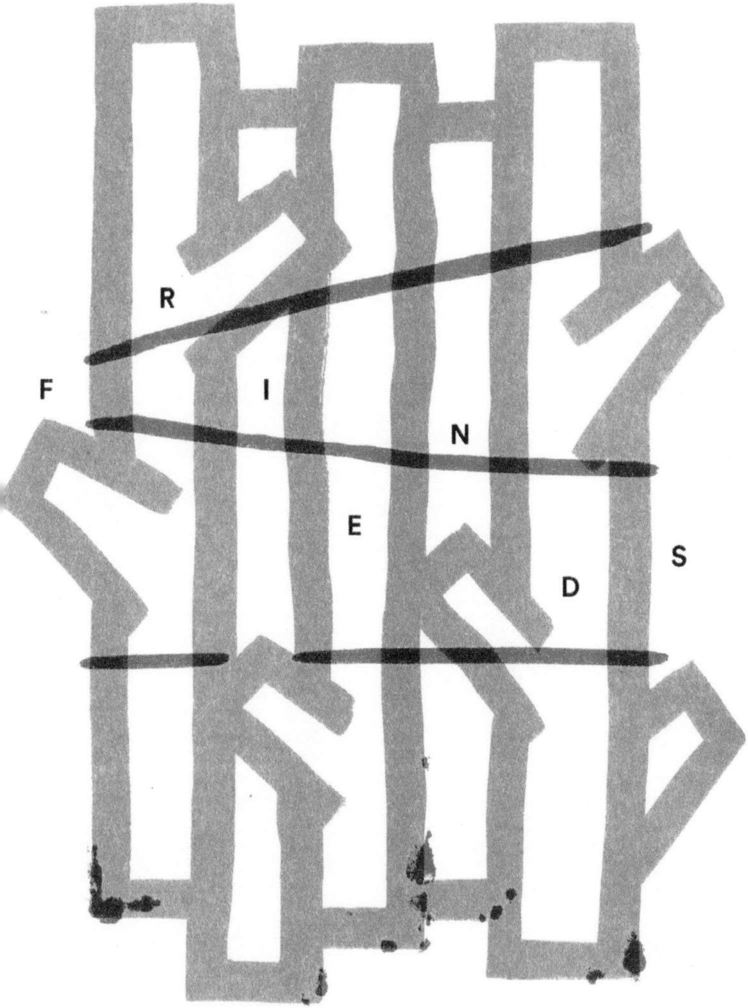
R
F
I
N
E
S
D

A

S O U L

L E A V I N G

A

B O D Y

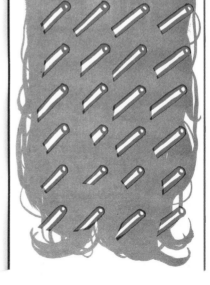

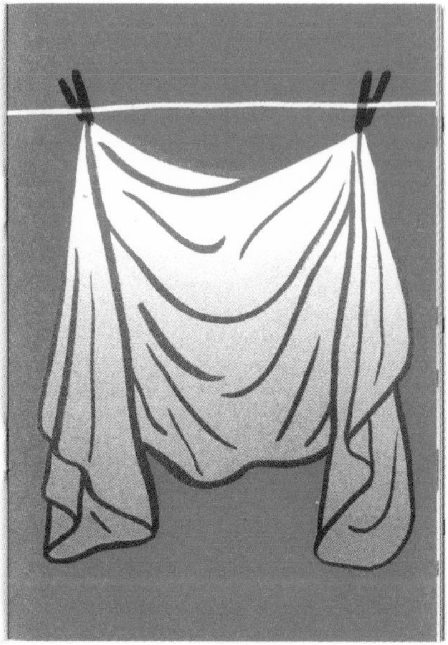

A   F

      F

E   C

           T

      I   O

                 N

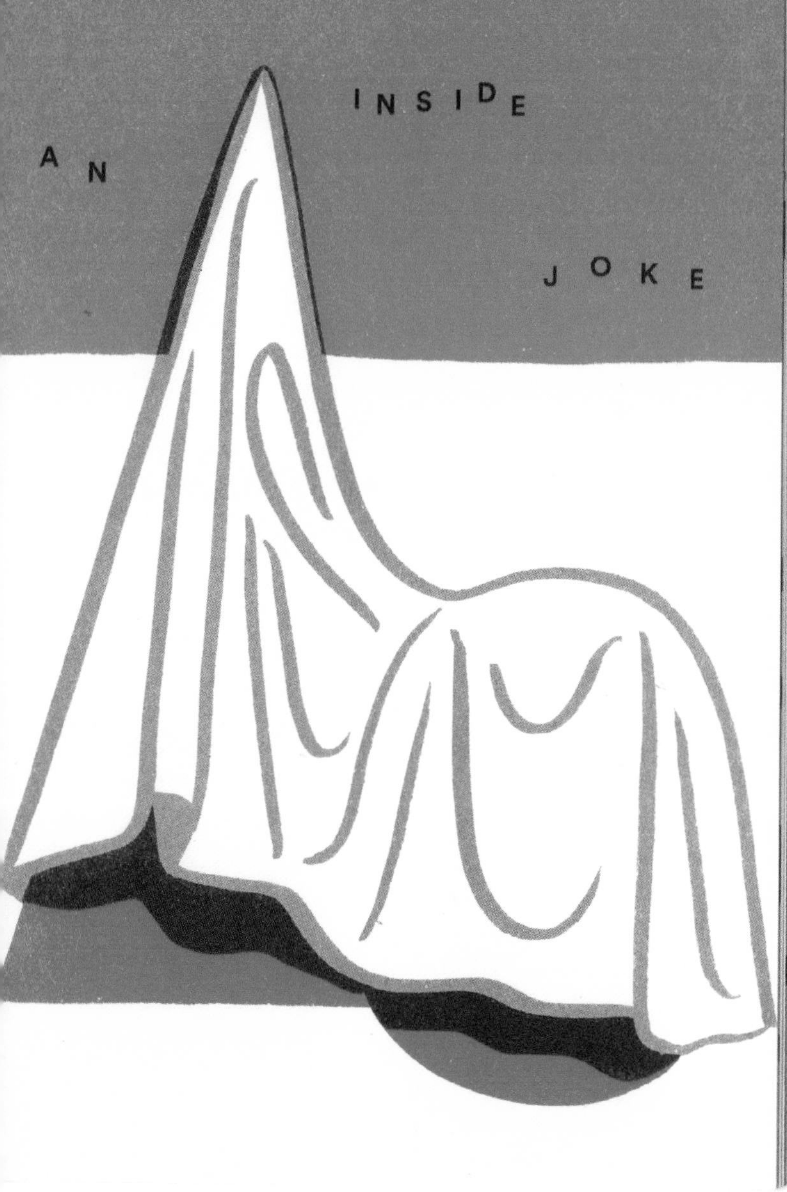
AN INSIDE JOKE

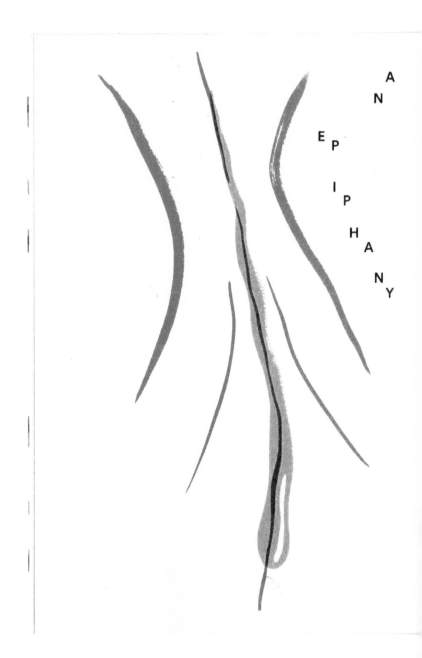

AN
EPIPHANY

T   M   I

A
T   T

R   C
A   T

I   O
N

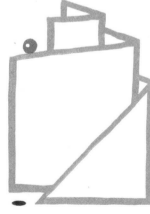

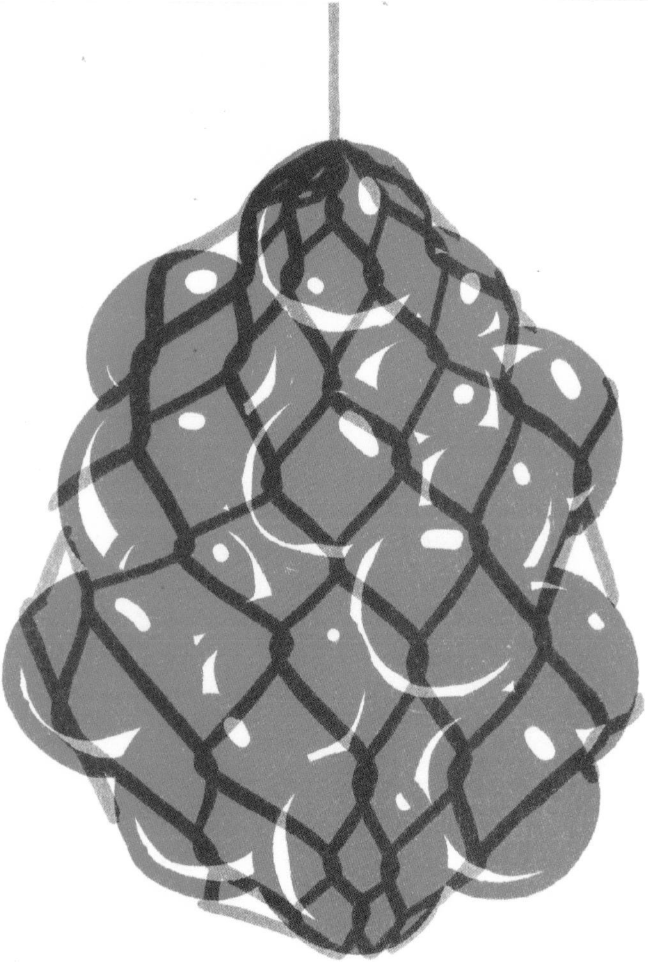

SECRETS

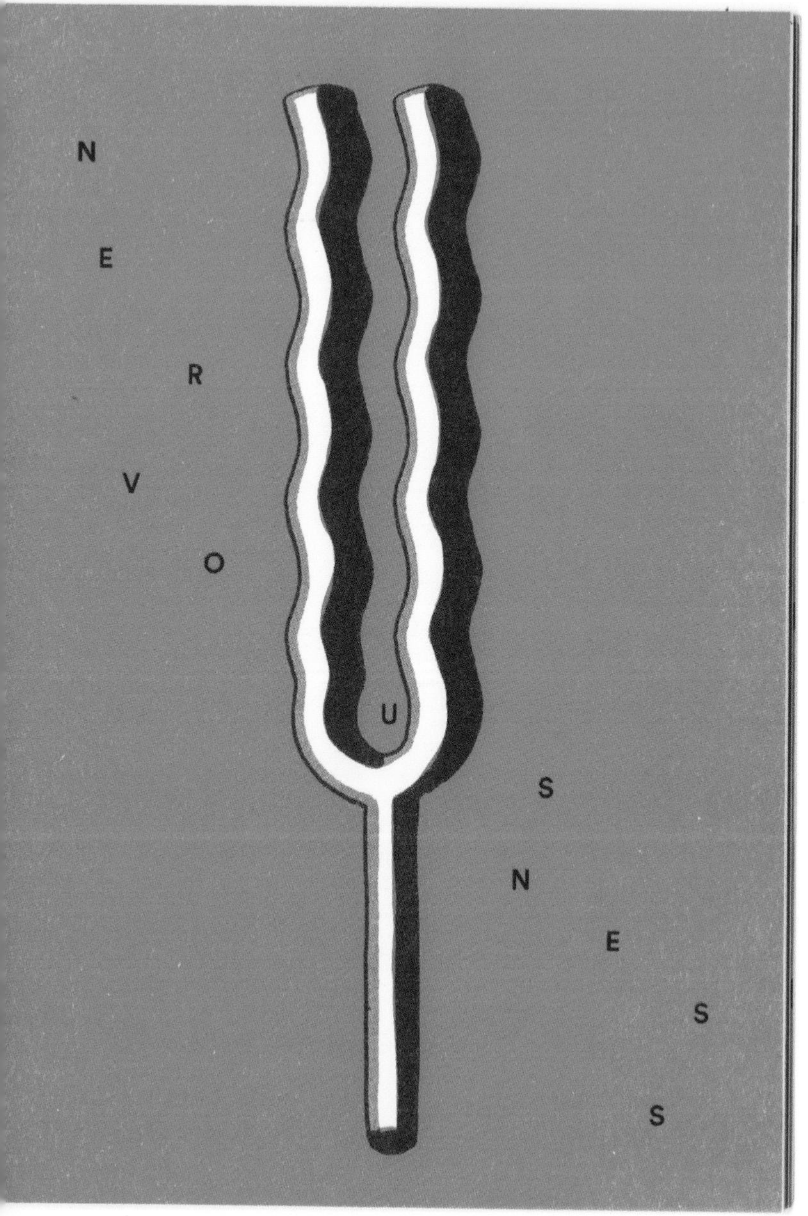
N E R V O U S N E S S

SEXUAL TENSION

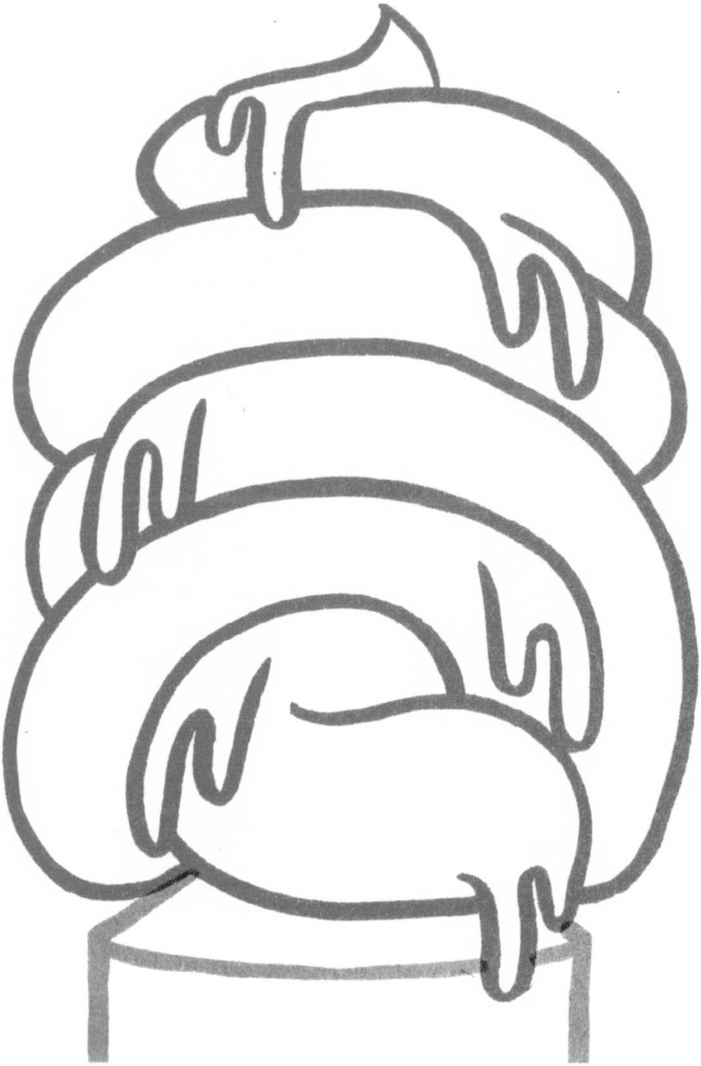

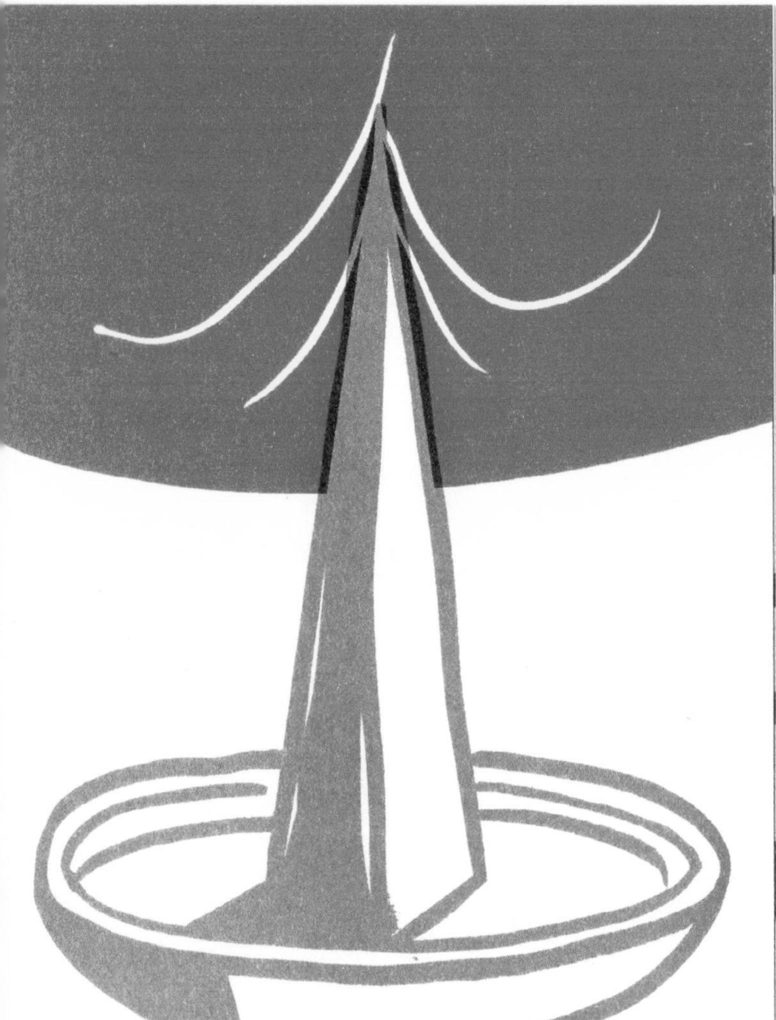

A LESSON

AN UNPLEASANT

TRUTH

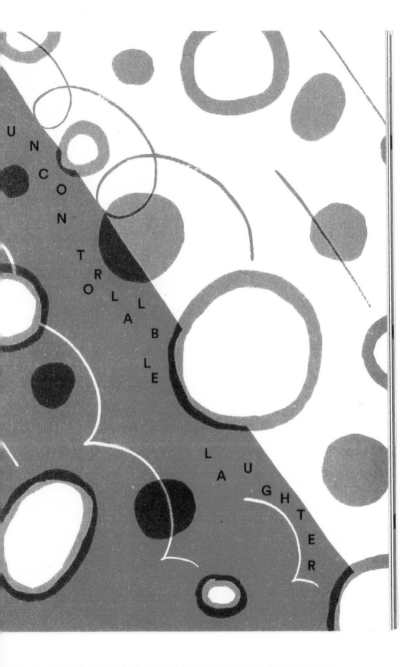

UNCONTROLLABLE LAUGHTER

SENTIMENT

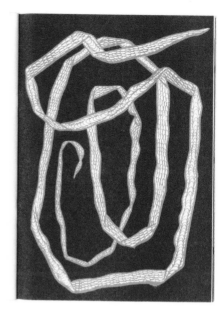

SETTLING

IN

YOUR

WAYS

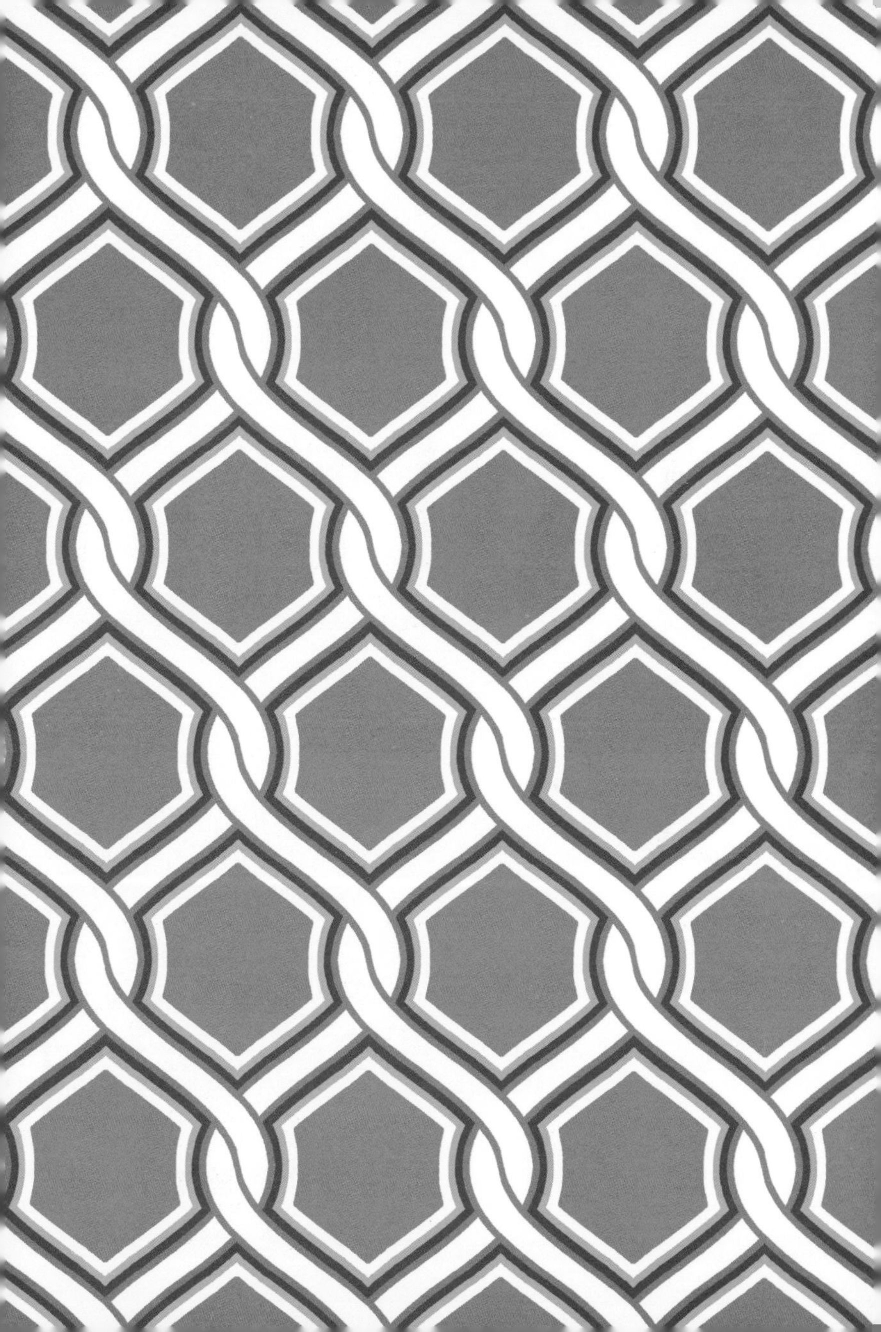

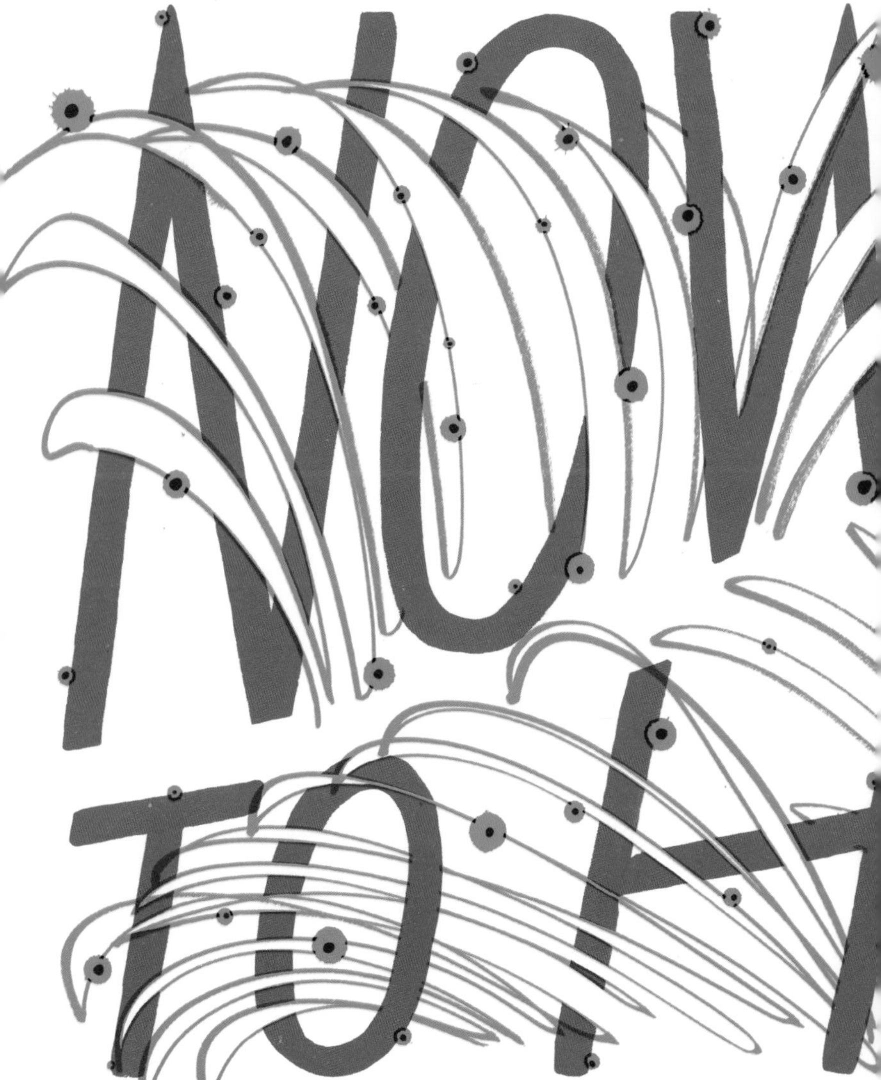

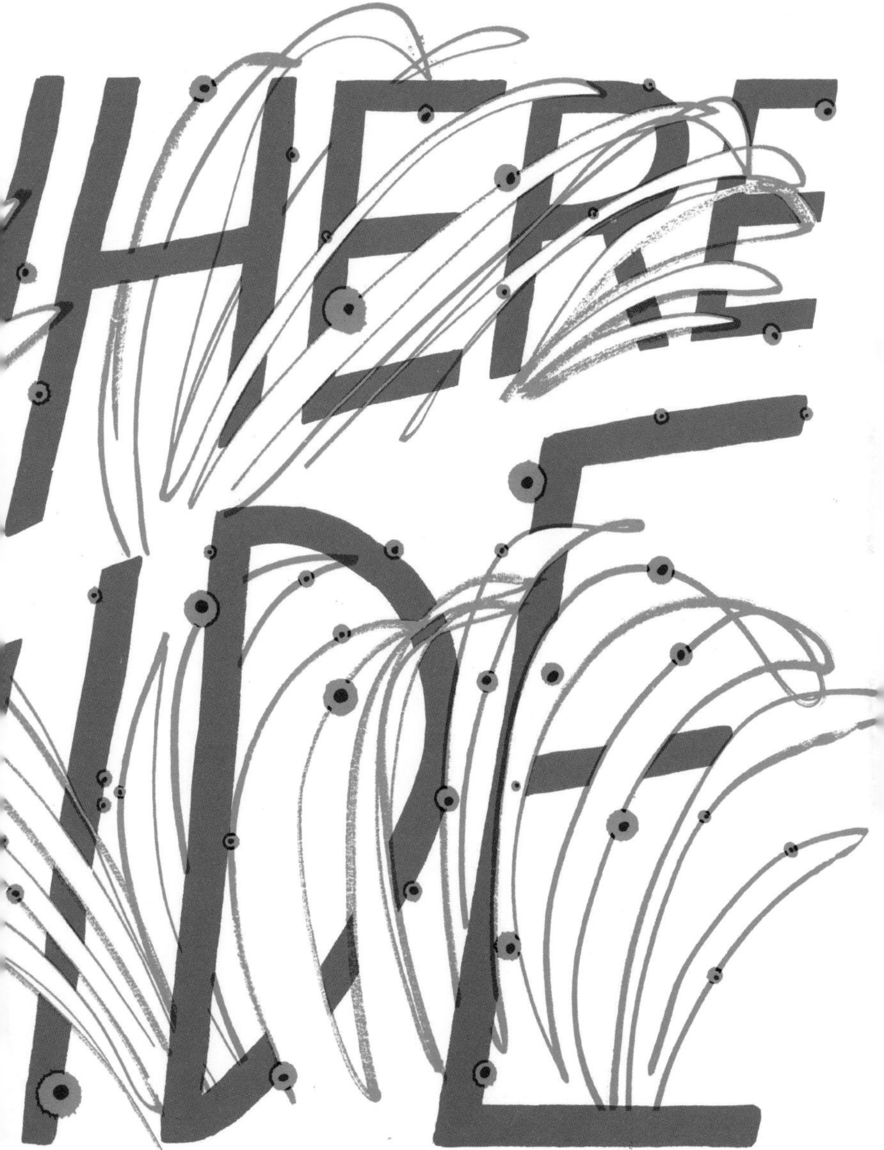

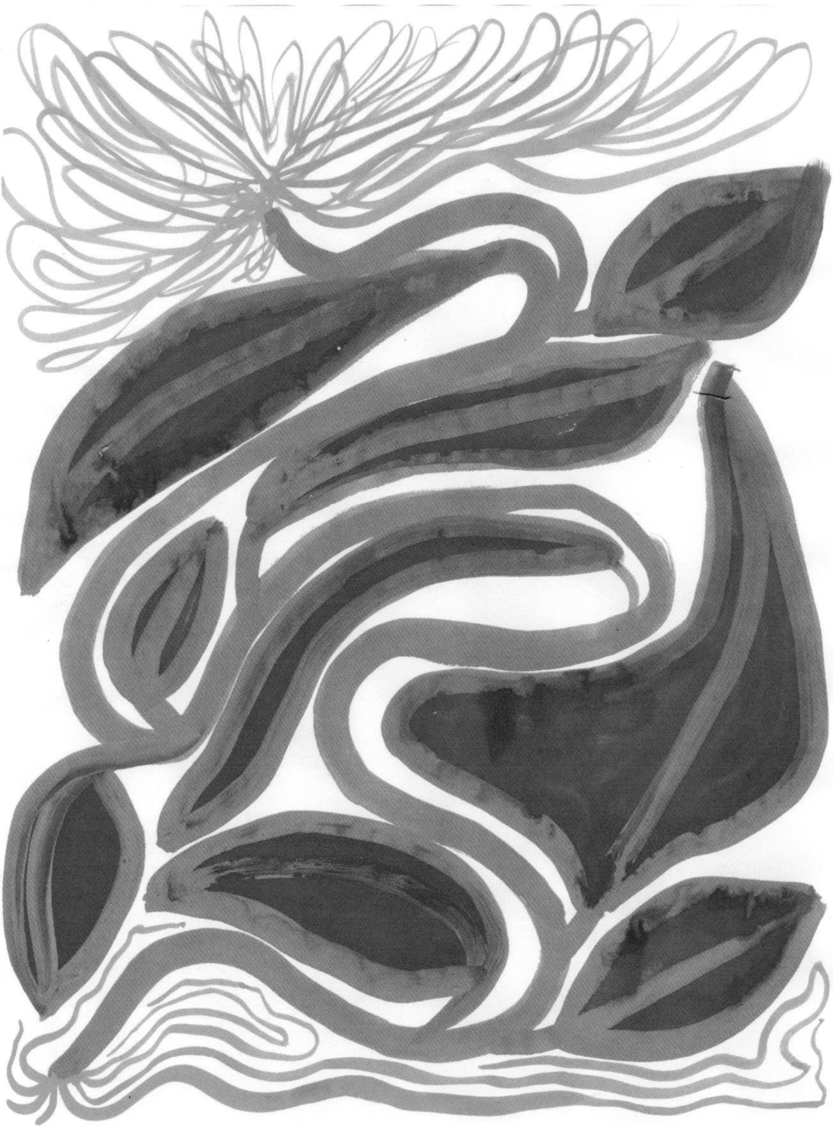

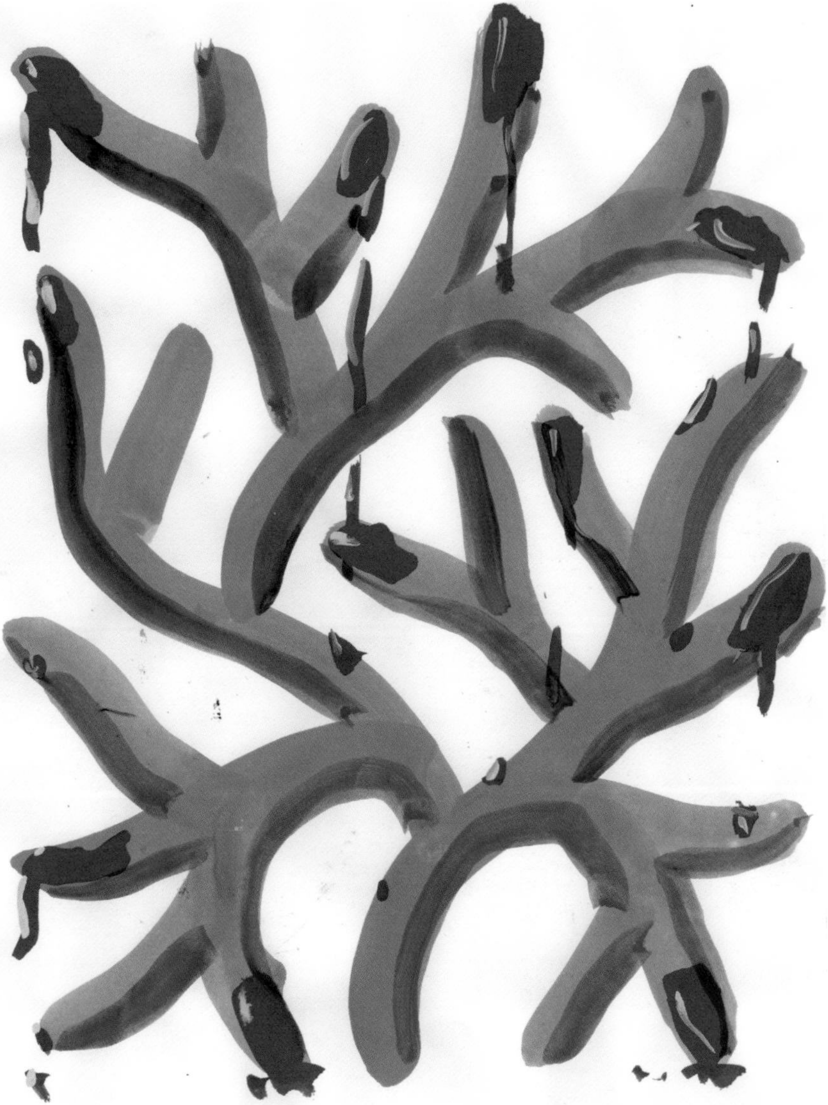

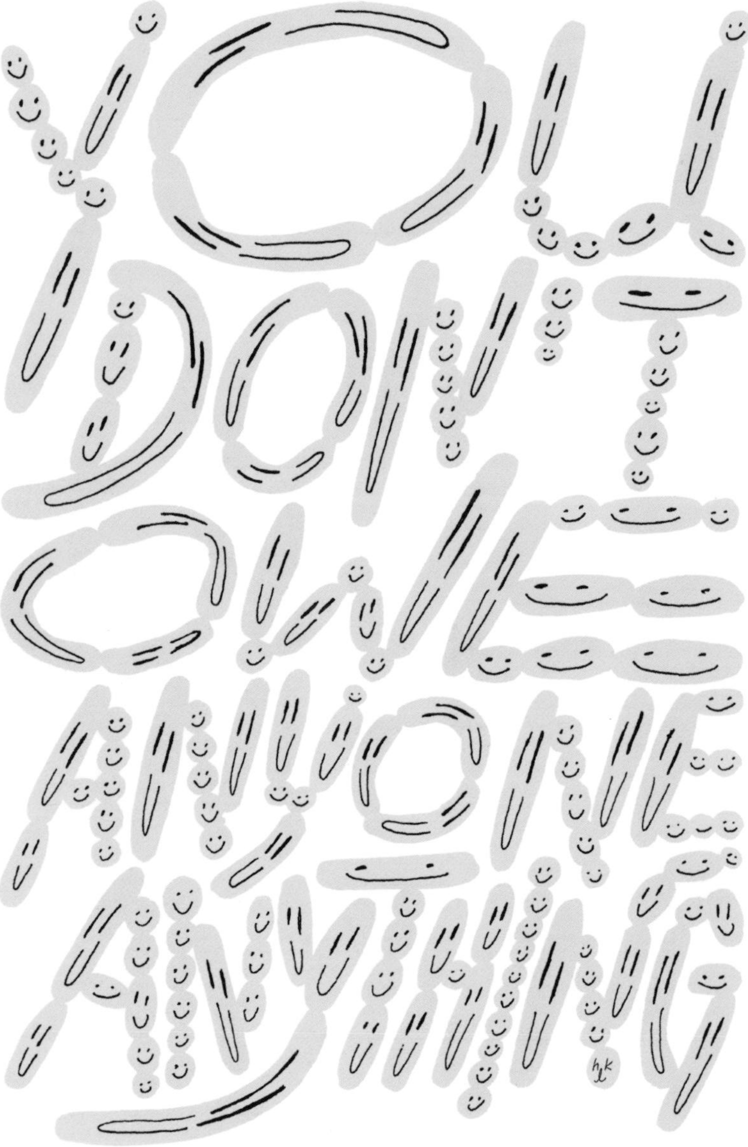
YOU DON'T OWE ANYONE ANYTHING

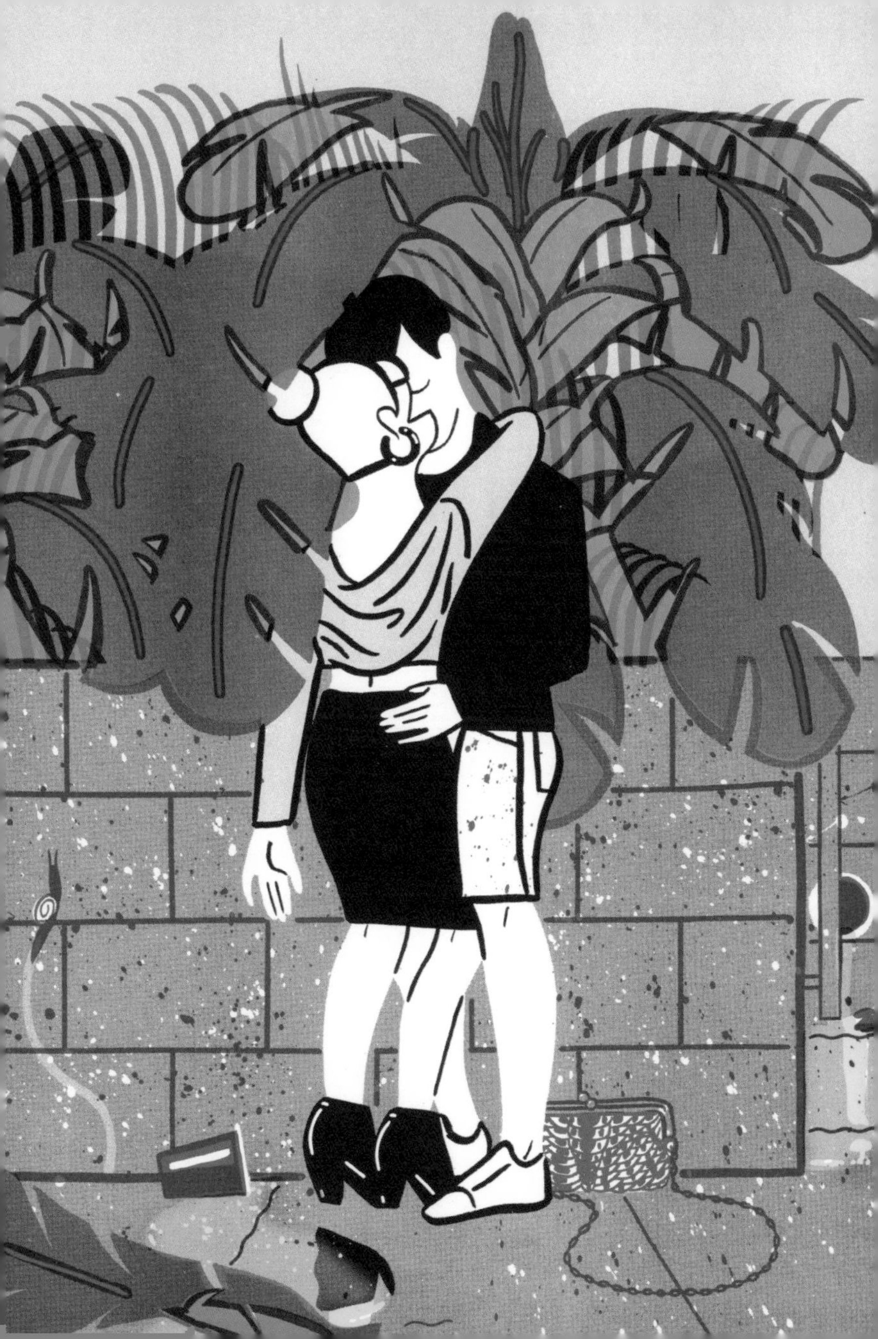

MILLE